The Digital Filmmaking
Handbook

Presents

I Got You Covered

The Premiere and Fun Guide to
Script Coverage, Notes, and Story Analysis

D1603244

Beverly Neufeld

Foreing Films Publishing | Los Angeles

The Digital Filmmaking Handbook Presents (series)
I Got You Covered (The Premiere and Fun Guide to Script Coverage, Notes, and Story Analysis)
Beverly Neufeld

Foreing Films Publishing

General Manager: Rainer Plain
Series Editor: Sonja Schenk
Editors: Sonja Schenk and Ben Long
Proofreader: Samura Adibzade
Interior Layout Tech: FF Inc.
Media credits:
All other images and media, copyright of Foreing Films Publishing

Library of Congress Control Number: 2022939125
ISBN-13: 978-1-7331502-3-1
ISSN 2690-0424

Foreing Films Publishing 3751 Motor Avenue, #1885, Los Angeles, CA 90034 USA

For product information and technology assistance, contact us at:
publisher@thedigitalfilmmakinghandbook.com
For permission to use material from this text or product, submit all requests via email to publisher@thedigitalfilmmakinghandbook.com

Visit our website at **thedigitalfilmmakinghandbook.com**

Acknowledgements

I will go in narrative order of how this came to be, from heart to product.

For support, love, and guidance: Lori Meyer, Michael Berman, Sharon Greene, Andrea Bensmiller, Katherine Wetherbee, Evan Hughes, Evan Neufeld, Jordan Ancel, Adam Kilbourn, Pete and Amy Huh, Debbie Salerno, Rona Solomon, Mike DeTrana, Steven Brandon and many more. It was a long journey from book proposal to book publishing, in which I lost three family members, and Covid hit, and they — and many more people — pretty much saved my life.

And of course, my cat, Prince Stanley Fuzzbucket (Fuzzy) Neufeld, who despite meowing constantly and walking over the keyboard and shedding all over it, makes my heart sing.

The biz:

It all began at UCLA with Meg LeFauve and her development class, and then Beth Greenwald, who got me my first development internship gig.

Peter Baxter and all the people at Slamdance Films, Jim Cirile and Anna Siri at Coverage Ink, the people at the Page Screenwriting Competition, and the many agencies and companies that hired, guided, advised, and trained me.

Forest Whitaker, Philippe Caland, and Nina Yang Bongiovi who hired and mentored me as a Development Executive at Juntobox Films.

Joey Tuccio at Roadmap Writers who hired me to teach my first coverage classes.

USC professors and amazing mentors, Jack Epps, David Isaacs, Kristen Wiley Davis, and many other professors for their beautiful hearts and wonderful words and guidance. However, those three initially hired me to teach the coverage class (and then multiple screenwriting classes) at USC. They brought me to a world I love and am grateful for every day.

My students at USC who taught me as much as I taught them, and a few who anonymously allowed me to use their coverage samples. Atul Sharma, a sweetheart who allowed me to use his review of my services.

For helping me with understanding what a book proposal even means: Jennifer Grisanti and Howard Suber.

Donald Hewitt, a fellow professor at USC, who generously introduced me to Sonja Schenk, who I'll get to in a moment, and Ben Long, who helped edit the book and made me much more succinct than I could ever be.

And finally, and most gratefully, Sonja Schenk, the world's nicest and sweetest publisher who took a chance on me, edited out the not-so funny jokes, worked her tushie off on this book, and helped guide my anxiety any time technology was mentioned.

Thank you all. You Got Me Covered.

About the Author

Beverly Neufeld received her MFA in Screenwriting from UCLA, went on to win numerous awards, started reading for competitions, coverage services, agencies, networks, and producers, and she also did private consulting. She was hired as a development executive and then as the Director of Development for Juntobox Films under Forest Whitaker and Nina Yang. After that she became a professor at USC's School of Cinematic Arts in their Writing Division, teaching script coverage and screenwriting classes and she also teaches online coverage classes.

She has been a script consultant for Slamdance Films, often speaking at their awards ceremonies and on panels for emerging screenwriters. She has also penned the letter they send out to finalists on how to capitalize on their momentum. Her coverage has caused many writers to seek her out repeatedly, and to hire her for rewrite assignments. On her own, Neufeld has also been hired on multiple scripts for rewrite assignments and has cowritten the film *Action! Action!*

The Digital Filmmaking Handbook Presents

I Got You Covered by Beverly Neufeld is part of the single-topic, companion-book series, *The Digital Filmmaking Handbook Presents*.

This series picks up where *The Digital Filmmaking Handbook* leaves off, tackling each topic exclusively, and as always, from the perspective of working filmmakers.

> *The Digital Filmmaking Handbook, 7th Ed* Ben Long & Sonja Schenk
> *Premiere Pro for Filmmakers* Sonja Schenk
> *I Got You Covered* Beverly Neufeld
> *Mastering the Short Screenplay* Donald H. Hewitt

Table of Contents

Foreward

Like many film school grads, I too, did my time as a script reader, writing coverage for Robert Altman's Avenue Pictures for twenty dollars a script. I later wrote coverage for a film distributor, screening independent film submissions for my boss who ultimately decided whether or not to take them on. When Beverly Neufeld approached me about writing this book, I was immediately interested because my own experience writing coverage has been invaluable.

Writing coverage requires the ability to look at a story that stretches forward in time over the course of an hour or more and be able to not only recognize why it works or how to improve it but also to successfully communicate these suggestions to people who have labored, often for years, on a project. Doing this is no small job and yet the position of story analyst, or reader, is often the place that a career in the film industry starts.

For new filmmakers, it's a great place to start because the crafting and honing of the story in films and series is a work in progress that begins with the script and gets revised with each hand that touches the project. I haven't written coverage myself in years, but I use my experience as a reader every time I evaluate a script as a director and each time I approve the final cut of an episode as a showrunner.

You'll find *I Got You Covered* by Beverly Neufeld to be a smart, savvy introduction to the practice of story analysis and the business that relies on it. Beverly's depth of knowledge and professional experience as a reader, screenwriter, development executive, and professor shine through on every page. Whether you intend to become a script reader or not, her book will help you acquire the skill of being able to think, write, and speak about the nuances of filmic storytelling, from script to screen.

Sonja Schenk
Publisher

Introduction

Since the beginning of time, cave people told stories and painted pictures on cave walls. And somewhere in the cave, amongst the hunters and gatherers and people working to invent wheels, there was always one person (let's call them "Blargh") who gave the story a thumbs up or thumbs down.

That's a critic. That's not what script coverage is about.

To the side of the campfire, hunched over and introspective, sat another cave person (we'll call them "Dirg") who suddenly leaped up and dashed over to the cave CEO. "Blurk. Blurk. Grunt," he said, with great excitement.

(Translation: "This story would work better if we make the lead role stronger and include three high-speed wooly mammoth chases.")

The CEO had many cave stories vying for their attention, and so they relied on Dirg to give a quick synopsis of each story and recommend which ones should be made into cave paintings. Dirg was the CEO's eyes and ears and the first "story gatekeeper." (Possibly before the invention of the first gate.)

Fast forward hundreds of thousands of years…

The flickering firelight has evolved into the flickering light of a projector, the stories have evolved to become much more complex, and the CEO…well, CEOs haven't really evolved much since their caveman days. But the script *reader* — the analyst and gatekeeper who helps the decision-makers in the entertainment industry — they're still here. Whereas a film critic gives an opinion about a finished product, a reader "covers a script," which means they analyze the script and assess whether or not it should go to the next level of consideration.

❓ What is a *Reader*?

A script *Reader* is the first person to read and consider whether or not a screenplay should be made into a movie. They receive screen or teleplay submissions, read them, and write reports. These reports, known as *coverage*, summarize and assess each script before sending it on to the next level, such as to a development executive, producer, agent, or studio executive. From this point forward, we'll capitalize *Reader* when referring to story analysts, as opposed to *readers* of this book.

ℹ️ Coverage

When Readers *cover* a script, they write analysis and reports for competitions, writers, or film executives. This often includes a synopsis, comments, a rating, and a decision to recommend that the script should go on to the next level.

What This Book Is About

I Got You Covered is an easy, fun, and comprehensible guide to script notes, critiques, and writing coverage for screenplays, teleplays, short films, and web series.

Whether you're reading this book to obtain a job, excel in your job, improve as a writer, and/or break through the gates of competitions, agencies, production companies, networks, and more.

I Got You Covered.

Whether you're starting as an intern or assistant, a person who wants to be a producer, development executive or literary agent, or you're a writer who wants to know what will make you stand out to competitions, agents, and execs... I got you covered.

Too often, writers receive script coverage or development notes from assistants and interns who have had little training in writing coverage. If the purpose is to ease the workload of their boss, then of course, how can the boss sit down and painstakingly explain to them what they need? They don't have the time — especially when rotating interns every quarter or semester. That's why I wrote this book: to help people understand the job and arrive already knowing how to do it so that they only need to learn the company's particular "language" or template when they start working. I got you covered.

Development or script notes are also given by development people, film and television executives, and sometimes also by marketing people who might understand the biz but not the show and could use a crash course in seeing the whole picture — of the picture they might want to fund. They may understand what to fix in order to market a project, but could spend some time learning more about the creative development process. And while most execs started as assistants, not all did. And of those who did, many were thrown into the deep end without a manual and learned some bad habits. Well, that cycle stops here. I got you covered.

And finally, notes are also given in writing classes and writer's groups. Such comments can either elevate or decimate the person receiving them. Many know the difference between criticism that guides a writer to enhance their vision and negative feedback that makes the writer want to quit and give up. Not on my watch. I got you covered.

I Got You Covered explores:

- Comprehensive breakdowns of the elements of a screenplay.
- How to spot a script's strengths and weaknesses.
- Methods to help elevate the weaknesses to equal the strengths.
- How to communicate criticism in a tactful, motivating, and inspiring way.
- How to remain objective rather than subjective.
- What competitions, executives, agents, networks, and Readers look for.
- Advice on getting your first job as a Reader.

What to Watch?

We'll use this monitor icon when we have movie viewing suggestions for you. Think of these suggestions as the best homework assignments ever.

Why Is This Book Needed?

I was hired by the Writing Division at USC's School of Cinematic Arts to teach this subject because their students apply for internships and assistant jobs so they need to be prepared to deliver good script coverage. As in the class, as you work through this book you will complete lessons, examples and assignments. In addition to teaching the details of script coverage, by the end of the book these assignments will also leave you with a portfolio and samples! In other words, this book can help you get work!

If you're a writer, you'll find additional benefit to reading this book. Back in film school, I learned a lot about all aspects of screenplay writing: breaking down complex and compelling stories and characters, assessing the marketability of a project, structuring a story to continually ramp up stakes and tension, and so on. Learning how to analyze screenplays made me a better writer. Many of my USC students have said they've heard things in writing classes for many years, but when they saw it from the point of view of executives, it made a tangible difference in their work.

By examining how coverage works and what Readers look for, writers will gain an edge in a very competitive market. Working as a professional Reader can be an invaluable experience for a writer. When analyzing a script, a writer can learn an immense amount from all kinds of scripts, "the good, the bad, and the ugly."

I've spent my life writing and helping writers. No matter what their level, everyone has a unique perspective and voice; I want to inspire people to find, hone, and express that voice.

I Got You Covered will reveal secrets on how to write a great script, how to make a script of any level better, what coverage is, how to give notes that inspire, how to leave your ego at the door, communicate better, and have fun while doing all these things.

And here and there I may include some lovely cat stories — not because cats are better than dogs — just funnier.

➡ More in *The Digital Filmmaking Handbook*

This book can stand alone but it was designed to work in tandem with *The Digital Filmmaking Handbook*. There you'll find a broad discussion of the role of the producer and how they develop ideas and pitches into series and films. There's also a chapter dedicated to screenwriting, including visual writing, three-act structure, and how to format a screenplay. Finally, it provides software recommendations for producers, writers, and directors.

In This Book

The book contains the following:

- **Chapters 1-2** provide an overview of what coverage is and isn't, who uses it and why, and some examples of templates that companies may provide.
- **Chapters 3-12** go over the different categories found in script coverage templates (such as genre, loglines, story, structure, etc.), what they mean, what employers specifically look for, and how to analyze and rate those categories.
- **Chapters 13-22** address various types of projects such as TV and books. We'll discuss tips and tricks on how to write coverage; how to work with writers, and we'll provide some career advice for those starting out as Readers and writers.

- **Exercises** found at the end of each chapter will help you understand the components of script notes, how to analyze screenplays, and how to write coverage.
- **Tales from my crypt:** throughout the book I include stories of personal experience working in "the business." I've learned a lot about reading (and writing) and hopefully my experiences can make that process easier for you.

So, if you want to become a Reader or you're a writer who wants to know how the gatekeepers work and how to improve your chances of getting past them… Welcome!

Dun… Dun… Dun… Roll opening credits…

1

Film Reviews and Coverage

What the Heck It Is & What the Heck It Isn't:
Rotten Tomatoes vs. Food for Thought

For the Glamour, Glory, and Gold?

What does a Reader or story analyst actually do? What gates do they actually keep?

When a writer submits their script to a *big company, network, or agency*, it first passes to a Reader who creates coverage. This coverage, along with the Reader's recommendation of whether the script should be considered or not, gets passed to the higher-ups.

If a writer pays for a coverage at a *screenplay service*, a Reader creates that coverage.

And when a writer enters a *screenwriting competition*, Readers are the ones who first assess the work. Many writers pay to enter a competition and only get a quick note or two. Others pay more to enter *and* receive coverage.

In some screenplay competitions, Readers judge the first round and then industry executives judge after that. But still, the Reader makes the first cut before it gets to people who could possibly help the writer's career. In other competitions, Readers judge all rounds.

Writers would love to know that they're first being read by agents, managers, and execs. They dream of their work being sucked up and out of the competition with John Q. Agent saying, "Who is this Writer McWriteyhead? I must contact them and become their rep!" However, when an agent or exec reads for a competition, just like in their regular jobs, they can't and don't want to read everything. So, they often judge the higher levels of a competition, thinking they'll see only the best — and they won't have to write notes because the Reader of the first round already did.

So, to recap: If a writer pays for notes in a competition, the Reader writes them. If their script is at a company, it goes to one of the company's Readers first. Either way, script Readers usually give projects one of three ratings:

- **Recommend**
- **Consider**
- **Pass**

So, Readers are pretty important. However, as of this writing, they still don't get the girls, glory, or gold.

So, Who Are These Readers?

Readers come in many shapes and sizes. Too often they come in larger shapes because they sit and read all day. About 95% (unfounded statistic — I'm just guessing) are or were writers themselves. Therefore, they should understand what a writer goes through and be able to speak "writer." Unfortunately, some have not been successful and might be a bit resentful or bitter. Many become Readers to learn how to make their writing better or because they want an "in" with a company themselves, and most do it for a supplemental income.

Ideally, Readers for execs and agents should be trained in doing coverage and have firm credentials, such as a degree from a film school, some sort of writing success, or have professional experience as Readers. Competitions and script coverage services do their own vetting, and each one has their own criteria for hiring Readers.

Readers employed by an agency, network, or production company can either be freelance Readers, or assistants and interns. Many interns are college students or are relatively new to the business, and yes — they read and judge writers' screenplays. Assistants often get their job because an agent needs someone to organize, schedule, type, and all of that — *and then* needs this person to also read and cover scripts.

What is the problem with that?

Well, some assistants are great assistants but not so great at coverage. They might not even want to write coverage. Sometimes they want to be a talent agent or a producer and start out "on the desk of" (an assistant to) a literary agent or development executive. They need to begin somewhere and make contacts, and while they believe that learning how to analyze a script will be helpful for whatever they do, that doesn't mean they're good at it. Many times, they're thrown into a company but not given enough training (a big reason I'm writing this book). And sometimes they're hired for political or nepotistic reasons and aren't that good at screenplay analysis. Yes, even though they may not be qualified they are still the ones who read and assess a writer's work and decide if it goes up the ladder or not.

What Do Readers Look for in a Script?

No matter where or for whom they work, a Reader is usually told what their company is/isn't looking for and they're often given the template their company uses. (I will go over some of those in the next chapter.) For example, a Reader at a radical feminist screenwriting competition will be told if the writer must be a radical feminist or if the script just needs to mention one. Independent film competitions may tell their Readers to look for a distinctive voice or message, and horror competitions want... well, horror (and sometimes thrillers). And if someone reads for a network like the Hallmark Channel, they wouldn't suggest they make *Get Out* because Hallmark has *very* specific guidelines on what they're looking for.

If an agency is looking to make a lot of money, they might prefer high-concept, big-budget projects, while independent companies will want smaller projects. And most companies and networks want what fits their brand. I was a development executive for a company that wanted to finance independent films. I sat at the Hollywood Pitch Festival and heard many great pitches. I hated that I had to turn down a historical drama (a genre I love) because that was beyond the budget of what we made. So, a Reader will not only be judging talent, but also how it fits with their company's needs.

Explain Yourself: Written vs. Verbal Notes

Most of the time Readers create written coverage. They're often given a template of what a specific company wants them to include, but on some occasions people give verbal notes.

For example:

- When I read for coverage services or do private consultations, sometimes I'm expected to *Skype*, *Zoom*, *FaceTime*, or call a writer and we go over the script.

- Executives give verbal notes to writers they've hired or are working with. I've done this as well.

- Sometimes the boss wants a Reader to tell them the notes verbally, but I don't find this to be the case too often. They usually want written copies for the company's database.

- Writers might give verbal notes when a friend asks them to read a script, or in writing groups or classes. And writing teachers and professors often give verbal notes to their students. Many writers will give and/or receive verbal notes at some point in their career.

There are many instances where one might need to give verbal notes, so I've devoted Chapter 19 to it. I'll go over the pros and cons of giving verbal notes in that chapter, as well as tips and dos and don'ts. But for now, let's focus on written coverage — which I separate into two categories: coverage created for the writer (that they will read) and coverage created for the executive (that the writer usually doesn't see). And when I say executive, I'll distinguish the different types of coverage required for agents, producers, and networks. (I will break down these differences and various templates in Chapter 2.)

There Is No *I* in Coverage

The main difference between a film review and script coverage is that the former is based on a final product, is the reviewer's opinion, and is often subjective. Coverage, however, is based on an unproduced script, is less of an opinion than an analysis, and must remain objective. The analyst must *represent* Readers, executives, or the audience and speak of the work objectively. This is true whether writing coverage for an executive, or coverage that goes directly to a writer.

I would not write:

> I think the story is a little slow.

Instead:

> The story seems a little slow.

I don't need to be mentioned. It makes it seem more subjective, and coverage should be objective and professional.

This is *especially* true when the coverage will be read by the writer directly because they could be very sensitive and more likely to dismiss what appears to be a specific person's thoughts.

For example, if I wrote:

> I'm confused by the main character's speech on page 10.

Perhaps an overly sensitive writer would dismiss this as that just my issue. However, if I take myself out of the equation and speak in broader terms, I might write something like:

> An executive reading this might get confused by the main character's speech on page 10.

I am indicating that it might not just be me, and I'm also letting the writer know that I'm on their side and want them to achieve their eventual goal — to win a competition, sell their script, get it made, and become a legend.

To recap: The main difference between writing a film review vs. a script coverage is:

> **A film review can be** *subjective*. "I loved Tom Cruise's performance and fanny pack."
>
> **Coverage is** *objective* — or at least it's supposed to be. "The protagonist needs to be more active by the end of Act One."

As audience members, most of us have analyzed movies and TV, and so have a rudimentary understanding of what should or shouldn't occur. Or at least, "what's good and what sucked about it." That's what film critics do, and I believe that examining our own opinions and checking out film and TV reviews is a good way to begin. Here are excerpts from examples of reviews:

Audience member Holly H's movie review on *Rotten Tomatoes* for the film *House of Gucci*:

> "I think that the 2 leading actors (Lady Gaga, Adam Driver) were both incredible and killed their roles, however the pace was very slow and strange. good movie tho go watch it yall its worth it"

Or Daniel Fienberg's *The Hollywood Reporter* review on the second episode of Peacock's *Bel-Air*:

> "Of course, without the *Fresh Prince* references, *Bel-Air* is almost entirely humorless, a chilly act of over-compensation. This is what happens when you attempt to call the bluff of a mock trailer that felt like it was intended to show Cooper's clever vision as a director, but not really as a proof-of-concept anybody wanted to see as an ongoing series."

Reviews can be casual or more formal, but reviewers often throw in their own voice, opinions, and a bit of sass. That's not what Readers do, but I highly recommend developing an understanding of movie reviews as a first step.

Read Some Movie Reviews

These are two sites to give you an idea on what reviews could look like: **vulture.com** and **rottentomatoes.com**.

Reviewing a Movie

When a person first leaves a film, they usually have some initial idea of what they did or did not like. That is where we start:

> It had cool car chases but otherwise it was sort of...
> meh.

The next step is for them to look at their feelings and analyze them. What was meh about it?

Start breaking the film down. We all have a sense about characters, pacing, logic, conflicts, and such, but we need to analyze the following when writing coverage:

> A. What are the elements that make a script good, bad, or meh?
>
> B. How can we help make it better?

The car chase example needs to be clearer. It can be more helpful if we point out what works and what doesn't and then offer reasons and suggestions for how to improve it. And we must do this without injecting our subjective opinions, talking in the first person, saying cruel and discouraging words, stating what *we* would do, or providing answers. It's also not helpful to throw five of our favorite movies at a writer and recommend that they go watch them. Whew.

So, rather than:

> It had cool car chases but otherwise it was sort of...
> meh.

Something I might write in an objective coverage of a script might be:

> The script has fast-paced action sequences and wonderful visuals. However, the characters could be further developed so that we are excited and more emotionally invested in their journey.

It's more formal, addresses the strengths, and goes into a possible weakness. I also show what could be gained by addressing the car chase issue. Note that the tone is professional. From here I would then go into specifics.

ℹ️ Page Count and Screen Time

Know that often one page = one minute of screen time. So, for example, the end of Act One usually occurs around pages 25-30, so that would be around the half hour mark.

Reading Scripts vs. Watching Movies

Note: To be a writer or a Reader, it's important to read scripts and not just watch movies and TV shows, since those are the finished product, not the "blueprint/script" that must first be sold, developed, and then produced.

It all starts on the page, and writers must convey as much as they can, as best they can, on that page — and Readers must analyze and assess that. Scripts, not films, come to literary agents, production companies, and competitions, so Readers must be familiar with them. Initially, reading scripts can feel jarring — plays can be read as literature, but scripts are meant to be *seen*. They are a visual medium, and we need to start reading *and visualizing* what's in them.

For example, become familiar with EXT. and INT. for *exterior* and *interior* shots.

        EXT. PETER'S HOUSE — DAY

... means we are outside.

        INT. PETER'S HOUSE — DAY

... means we are inside.

We also need to know the difference between stage directions that could be shot and translated to the screen:

        She picked up her mother's wedding photo.

Versus:

        She thought back to how great last year
        was. She remembered her mother's smile
        fondly.

We can't see inside of a character's head. That's a luxury that novel writers have that script writers don't. In a script, writers must convey what we see and hear and what people do. Too often they put in internal thoughts, feelings, or backstory — things that can't be shown.

For example, instead of:

```
Amelia looked at the school. She had just
transferred there and didn't know
anybody.
```

We might have another character see Amelia, looking lost, and ask:

```
                MORGAN
        Hi. Are you new?
```

We can see and understand that.

 ## Screenplay Resources

Make sure to get familiar with screenplays, both good and bad. The following is a link to the top ten screenplay databases: **nyfa.edu/student-resources/10-great-websites-download-movie-scripts**. And: **scriptreaderpro.com/best-screenplays-to-read**. I also recommend **scriptslug.com** as they have many new screenplays. I suggest reading ones that were nominated for or won screenwriting awards, since most often they nailed it on the page.

Exercises

Watch a movie. Later we'll look at other forms, such as TV shows — but for now, make it a movie. It can be in a theater or on a streaming platform like Netflix, Amazon, or Hulu but it should be a feature — something approximately 1 ½-2 hours long. Enjoy it without taking notes, just as you'd do as an audience member.

Now, write a movie review. Try the following:

1. Summarize the movie as best you can, in no more than three paragraphs. Notice what you include and what you don't. What sticks in your head?

2. Analyze and critique the film but as a reviewer. Be subjective, use *I*, get passionate, exasperated — all the things we'll unlearn later when writing coverage. Aim for about a one-page written review.

3. Rate the film, perhaps from 1-10 with 10 being the highest mark. Would you recommend it to others?

Get your subjective feelings out first. We'll then learn how to translate them to objective comments and suggestions. The point is to first see what you think and feel and then break it down to see why you feel the way you do — both the good and the bad. We start this way and then we'll pull back on our passion, venom, envy, resentment, and so on, so we can analyze projects objectively. Good luck. I believe in you.

The show manages to skillfully talk about bullying and mental health amongst teenagers in a funny and self-aware manner. The script has very colorful characters, who all feel very realistic for a satire. The lead is strong and extremely empathetic. She truly is the embodiment of most teenagers, and her angsts are their angsts. There is a lot to like here, but a few minor things to be tweaked in order to make this a hit show. The exposition is poorly delivered, with some dialogue that seems written simply to deliver information to an audience, on top of a diary, and dream sequences. Those lines need to be more skillfully integrated into the story, and the exposition needs to come more naturally or through conflict. On the other hand, the dialogue is strong in regard to the comedic genre. It is very quick and witty, with some gems that will be added to the audience's vocabulary. Structurally, the script is simple, but works. A lot has been planted for future episodes, and a whole world is there. Nonetheless, the pilot moves at a fast pace with rising stakes, finishing up with a solid and unpredictable hook. For the plot of the pilot, it would be beneficial to further focus on the lead character's relationship with other characters, instead of spending so much time on some seemingly less important secondary characters, like the teachers. This being because although, as mentioned, the pacing works, to further explore the lead might further cement the audience's engagement with the show, given how so much of the script is dedicated to plants for future episodes. Another moment in the plot that needs restructuring is when JD shows up at Veronica's house and pushes for the whole revenge plan. It is a key moment in the story, but in the current version it seems forced into the story just because the plot point needs to happen, and it's not earned. Characters-wise, the show's main antagonist, Heather Chandler is the most two-dimensional character in the pilot, with no indications of who she is and why, nor of what she wants. This seems to work in this short pilot and the audience needs to hate her, and given that she does not die, there is the opportunity to further develop her in future episodes. In contrast, the lead character is fully fleshed out, especially for a character that is supposed to be "ordinary." Her likability is high, and she is the perfect character to attract big talent. The tone of this script seems in tune with the preferences for today's youth, and it does offer a lot of valid commentary on society. This series does require a network that is not afraid of some backlash, given that through humor it makes light of teenage suicide and has jokes about being fat, gay, and much more. Some members of the audience might not understand the liberal leaning politics of the show and misinterpret these as conservative attacks. Overall, the project does have the added benefit of carrying the name of the cult classic movie, automatically having an audience of fans. On top of that, there are no shows out there with a similar tone, setting this one apart. Comedic tone, realistic and engaging characters and a pilot that sets out a season to come.

2

Templates from the Trenches

Examples from Buyers, Competitions, and Services. This Is What They Want!

There are two basic types of written coverage. Coverage that goes directly to the screenwriter and coverage that goes to people who work in the development of film, series, and other entertainment projects.

- **Coverage for writers** is usually *comment-heavy* and *synopsis-light*.
- **Coverage for agents and executives** is usually *synopsis-heavy* and *comment-light*.

What does that mean? Read on…

Developing Entertainment

Development is the term for acquiring a script, shaping the story, and preparing the script for shooting. Development can start with an idea, a developed treatment or pitch, or a completed script, and end with a screen or teleplay ready to go to directors, actors, producers, casting directors, etc.

Development executives at companies find, assess, and develop ideas or scripts into projects. They work to create new drafts of a screenplay by giving notes to the writer, bringing on new writers for rewrites, and attaching key players such as directors, other producers, and actors. Development is the phase of filmmaking that happens before pre-production begins.

The normal process of production includes the following stages:

- **Development:** Idea to finished script.
- **Pre-Production:** Preparing to film (casting, hiring, financing, legal issues like getting permits, scouting locations, etc.)
- **Production:** Shooting/filming a project and all that entails.
- **Post-Production:** Editing, honing, shaping, etc. (Getting it "in the can" and ready to sell or show)
- **Marketing and Distribution:** Selling, advertising, promoting and showing. (How does it get to theatres and other platforms? How do you hear about it?)

On both sides of a film production deal, *sellers* (agents and managers) and *buyers* (development execs, producers, network execs, and so on) receive piles and piles of scripts. So sellers hire Readers to sift through all the submissions that come to them. When sellers (or even writers directly) submit projects to buyers, the buyers also have Readers. So, Readers can be hired to do coverage for either a buyer or a seller.

Often it may look like this:

- A *writer* writes a script.
- Writer submits it to a seller, i.e., an *agent* or *manager*, to get considered as a client.
- *Agent or manager's Reader* reads submissions, writes coverage, and recommends which project or writer the agent should take on.
- *An agent* signs the writer and sends their script out to a possible *buyer, production company, network,* or *studio* where it usually goes to the *development execs* there. (Some agencies must have a few agents agree before signing a new writer.)

- *The exec's reader* sifts through submissions, writes coverage, and recommends which projects the exec should read. The exec can then send the script up to *their bosses.*

There are many exceptions to this process. Sometimes agents and managers will *hip pocket* a writer, meaning they may not sign them but will represent one of their projects. Sometimes writers are able to give their work directly to the development people. Also, a writer might sell a *pitch* (the idea) and then get hired to write the script.

Gatekeeping: Covering for an Executive (In More Ways Than One)

For most people, this is the type of reading job they're looking for — or the only one they knew was out there — writing coverage for some sort of development executive in some sort of company.

Earlier we explained the difference between buyers and sellers. A studio may be looking for projects for their main star, an agency may be looking for new writers or something a client can direct, a network may be looking for shows that fit their brand, etc. However, one thing that applies to all is that they need Readers as their gatekeepers. Each company will tell their Readers what they're looking for and most will provide a custom template for script coverage.

Busy agents and producers rely on coverage to quickly get the concept of a script and to judge how well it is written. This is why I say that trust is important. They must trust a Reader to know the market, know what they (these execs) want, report what the project is about, report how well it was written and what (if anything) might be needed to improve it, and let them know if it's worth their time to read or not. Since these execs want to make money, they are often interested in characters' age, gender, ethnicity, and descriptions for casting; as well as setting, budget, and more.

All executives get more script submissions than one can imagine. They can't read them all, so they rely on Readers to cut their workload, summarize and comment on scripts, and pass, consider, or recommend the project. That's right. Sometimes the buck stops with the Reader, the mighty gatekeeper. Oh, the power!

So, for all executives *the summary or synopsis is very important.* They usually don't want pages of comments - just overall assessments. They need the Reader to convey the story succinctly. They also need to know how well it was written but they also know they can have it rewritten, so they'll read the synopsis to see if they're interested and read the Reader's comments to see if it's good. If they get to the point where they read it themselves, they'll make their own notes.

The purpose of coverage for an executive is to discern *if they should read that particular project or not*. Remember, their question is, "Will this make money?"

Here are some types of executives who use coverage:

Agents

There are many types of agents but the two a Reader will most likely deal with are *literary agents*, who represent writers, and sometimes *talent agents*, who represent actors and directors.

Readers mostly do coverage for literary agents and read scripts for three reasons:

- Determine if the agent should consider representing this writer or project.
- Cover a new script written by one of their existing clients.
- Summarize a script so that it seems like the agents read it. *Talent agents* might also request coverage for clients they represent. For example, if an agent represents a hot director or actor, they want to know if this project would be right for that client. Don't worry, Readers are usually filled in on what all these people are looking for.

For example, a literary agent may be looking for big budget studio movies because they don't want to make small, "independent film" money, which may also be harder to sell. And perhaps a talent agent may want to find an Oscar-worthy project for their action star.

Producers

Producers and production companies also have Readers looking for projects for their companies. Disney and horror movie companies want very different projects. Some companies have deals with certain studios or networks, and quite a few are run by actors and directors who are looking for vehicles to either star in or helm.

Most of these companies have development departments and executives who hire Readers to scout for the kind of projects they like to do. This differs from competitions, coverage services, and agents who will look for various types of projects.

Distributors of Original Content

As with producers and production companies, most networks seek out projects that serve their distinctive brands. For example, FX would want something different than HBO, and premium cable has different requirements than broadcast networks. There are also different rules for various streaming platforms, half-hour vs. hour-long shows, etc.

Consider the problem of a broadcast network that has a nice Thursday comedy line-up and wants something to fit the 8:30 time slot. It has to fit in and appeal to the same demographic that watches the shows that come before and after, must be clean enough for broadcasting when some children are still up, be funny, and fit the half-hour format, including commercials since broadcast networks rely on ad sales for profit.

A one-hour drama on a broadcast network shown at 10 pm can be a bit more adult, since they assume kids are asleep (ha, what do they know?). But since it's still a broadcast network that relies on ads, it can't be too vulgar, gritty, or edgy. It must also go with the network brand and fit in a one-hour time slot with commercials.

Premium cable networks like HBO or Showtime rely on subscribers so they can be edgier. Viewers tune in for what they can't see on regular broadcast networks. Their shows need to fit the 30- or 60-minute standard (unless it's a movie) without commercials. Some cable stations like FX offer fare between broadcast and premium cable in terms of content and also have commercials.

At the time of this writing, streaming is the Wild Wild West. Since people watch on demand, at any time, scripts can be 45 pages (like 45 minutes), 48 pages, 75, etc. Some platforms have commercials, and some don't. Some have brand mandates (like Disney+) or don't (Netflix presents: *Bridgerton, Tiger King, Big Mouth, Dear White People*, etc.)

Help Is on the Way: Coverage for a Writer

Most people might prefer reading for agents, producers, and executives and some might not even know that creating coverage for a writer is an option. Surprise! Not only are there multiple paid opportunities to pen coverage for writers, but it's also a good way to start. Coverage for writers is quite different than coverage for executives — and often more rewarding.

Writers pay Readers to help them improve their screenplay, so the Reader's job is not to tell the writer what *they themselves* would do, but rather, how to get *the writer's writing* in the best shape possible. Writers can be sensitive or defensive, so the Reader's tone really matters. If the Reader is only supplying written coverage without an accompanying call or consultation, then they must be very clear on the page. Writers often seek out coverage to help them improve their scripts. They may also have blind spots and want feedback before sending their darlings out to the bigwigs.

Earlier I said that coverage for writers is usually *comment-heavy and synopsis-light*. This means that writers don't need a long synopsis of what their work is about. They know. When creating coverage for a writer, commenting on execution is our most important task. What works, what doesn't, and how can we help them improve it? How is their story going? What about their characters, the tone, structure, etc.? (I will address all of these categories and more in the following chapters.)

Writers seek coverage in three ways...

Script Consulting Services

Script services offer coverage to writers — and hire many Readers. There are tons of script service companies out there and many are quite good, but did I mention... there are tons? So, the odds are that a few aren't great. This could be bad news for a naïve writer who pays big bucks to a subpar company, but good news for a prospective Reader — it means that there are numerous job opportunities. Many script consulting services are also associated with competitions and I'll get into those next.

A writer usually pays the script coverage service who then takes a cut (the amount varies) and sends the script to one of their Readers (who gets the rest of the money). These companies handle all the marketing, give out assignments, and stand between the Reader and the writer. They are intermediaries so writers can't contact the Reader directly. This means that if a writer has positive or negative feedback about the coverage their script received, they'll have to send it to the company who will then forward that feedback to the Reader. The Reader represents the company so it's in their interest to address any complaints.

Some coverage service companies include:

> *Coverage Ink*
> *Coverfly*
> *WeScreenplay*
> *Script Reader Pro*
> *Roadmap Writers*

(I've worked for two of the above but won't tell which, to remain mysterious. Shhh.)

When I read for script consulting or coverage service companies, the services could be year-round or seasonal. For example, the Slamdance Screenplay Competition runs from around March to September each year. I will receive an email with an assignment (a script to cover) and a deadline. This is a service *for writers* and the coverage will be read *by writers*. One or two of these services ask their Readers to be a bit more sympathetic in their coverage, since it's not about buying, selling, or winning. The purpose of the coverage is to help and guide a writer.

Screenwriting Competitions

Most writers enter screenwriting competitions hoping just to enter and win, but many pay extra to enter and receive coverage. Their screenplay is judged to see if it should advance or not, but then they also get notes, just like with coverage services.

There are multitudes of screenwriting competitions, so just like with coverage services, some are reputable, and some aren't. And again, the contest companies act as brokers — getting the submissions, taking a cut, and doling out assignments. They also forward any complaints or praise the writer gives, and the Reader's work helps or hinders their reputation.

The top (long standing, vetted and most respected) ones include:

> Academy Nicholl Fellowships
> Page International Screenwriting Awards
> Austin Film Festival Screenplay Competition
> Coverage, Ink
> Slamdance Screenplay Competition
> Sundance Screenwriters Lab
> Scriptapalooza
> Script Pipeline
> ScreenCraft
> Final Draft Big Break

(I've also worked for three of the above. Shhhh.)

There are many similarities between script coverage services, and screenplay competitions. Writers who enter competitions and also pay to receive coverage will also see the coverage directly and want notes to help them improve. Competitions are usually seasonal, and the biggest difference between competitions versus coverage services is: *The writer hopes to advance and then win.*

So, Readers for competitions also rate the script:

> **Recommend/Consider/Pass**
>
> Or
>
> **Advance/Doesn't Advance**

Many script competitions also give a *short form* of coverage for all who enter. This is usually a logline, maybe a quick summary, and a paragraph of the overall strengths and weaknesses.

Private Consultations

A private consultation is when a writer pays a Reader for coverage and there's no intermediary. To get jobs like this, a Reader must either put themselves out there and market themselves or when they're good — sit back and writers will come and find them.

Over the years, thanks to all the companies I've worked for and writers I've met, I've been hired to do private coverage a lot. It's the bees' knees! A Reader can make their own rules and templates, work more directly with writers, no one takes a cut, and can charge what they think is appropriate.

❓ What If I Have No Notes?

Some Readers may worry, "What if a script is great and I have no notes?" I think that's a great problem to have. If a writer pays for coverage and gets minimal notes, wouldn't that be encouraging? I mean because it was good — not that the Reader was lazy and they paid a lot of money just to be told, "Looks good, bro'."

Examples of Templates

In many cases, companies provide a template for what they're looking for in the way of coverage. Not all do, but regardless, on the following pages are some templates I have worked with, to provide a sense of what many are seeking.

Screenwriting Competition Coverage Report

Here is a simple coverage template for a screenwriting competition that would be seen by a writer.

READER INITIALS: *Put in your initials.*

TITLE OF SCREENPLAY: *Insert title.*

TRACKING ID#: *This is usually provided by the company.*

ADVANCE   DOESN'T ADVANCE

Underline one or the other or put one in bold. But does it advance in the competition? Can it be a finalist?

<u>FEEDBACK FOR ENTRANT</u>: *Don't write anything on this line. It just states that the writer will see everything below.*

GENRE: *What is the genre?*

LOGLINE: *Give a one or two sentence logline.*

THREE TO FIVE SENTENCE FEEDBACK: *This is your intro —
the main points you will discuss in the comments section. State
the overall strengths and then the weaknesses. Ex:* This is
exciting, original, and very imaginative. The world is fascinating,
and the details are incredible. There are big obstacles and high
stakes. The main issue seems to be one of clarity and context.
We need to go deeper into the characters, their relationships,
and backstories to emotionally invest more in their journey.
There are also many surreal elements that need clarifying.

SHORT SYNOPSIS: (One paragraph): *Capitalize new
characters. Since this is short (only a paragraph) do it after
reading and just convey the overall plot/facts. This is for the
writer. They know what they wrote.*

SCREENPLAY ANALYSIS/COMMENTARY (about 1-2 pages in
paragraph form, of notes): *Here's where your main notes are
given — in essay form. You can refer to page numbers to give
examples or for things you "bump up against." Watch your tone
(we'll go over that in Chapter 17) and guide them on how to
improve it. Do not use I or me or address the writer directly.*

RECOMMENDATIONS (conclusion, last remarks): *Don't bring
up new points. This is the conclusion or summation of what you
already said. Often, in this category I might break down the
steps for a rewrite and reassure them that it's not a lot of work .
Leave on an encouraging note.*

More Templates in the Appendix

I have included three additional examples of script coverage
templates in the Appendix at the end of this book: a more detailed
script competition template, a network series template, and
something I came up with, a template for private consultation with
a writer.

Coverage for a Large Agency

This is the type of coverage template a writer might receive from an agent.

Title: Insert Title.

Writer: *Insert the writer's (or writers') name(s).*

Studio: Studio/Financed Independent/Independent *They will
inform you if any studios are attached.*

Prod Company: *They will inform you if any companies are
attached.*

Producers: *They will inform you if any producers are attached.*

Draft Date: *Month/Day/Year it was written. N/A if not included.*

Pages: *How many pages (not including the title page).*

Genre: *What genre is it?*

Time: *Name all time periods.*

Location: *Name all main settings (ex: NYC, not "A living room").*

Reader: *Your name.*

Date: *Month/Day/Year of coverage.*

LOGLINE: *Give a one or two sentence logline.*

PREMISE: *In this case, premise doesn't mean concept. Here, they want a shorter version of the synopsis.*

SYNOPSIS: *This is where, in paragraph form and third person, you tell the story of the script, hitting the important facts, so they can understand it and engage. And just like with a screenplay, all new characters are introduced in capital letters with ages given. This helps them keep track of people for the story and for possible casting. Summarize the plot for them. They have not read it.*

COMMENTS: *Here's where your main notes are given — in essay form. You can refer to page numbers to give examples or for things you "bump up against." Watch your tone (as we'll go over in Chapter 17) and inform the agent about the project's strengths and weaknesses, as well as its possible potential. Do not use I or me and do not address the agent directly.*

Concept/Originality: EXCELLENT/GOOD/FAIR/POOR

Characters: EXCELLENT/GOOD/FAIR/POOR

Dialogue: EXCELLENT/GOOD/FAIR/POOR

Structure: EXCELLENT/GOOD/FAIR/POOR

Format: EXCELLENT/GOOD/FAIR/POOR

Script: RECOMMEND/CONSIDER/WEAK CONSIDER/PASS

This is where you rate each category by underlining one of the choices or using bold font.

Sample TV Pilot Coverage

This third example is from a generous and wonderful student's sample coverage on the produced TV pilot, *Heathers*.

TITLE: Heathers
WRITER: Jason Micallef
SUB BY: N/A

SUB TO: N/A

FORM: Half Hour comedy TV Pilot.

PAGES: 34

ELEMENTS: N/A

READER: XX

LOGLINE: An ordinary high school student fed-up with the popular kids' reign on the school, unites with a rebel and psycho new kid to prank the school's Queen B. Once that goes wrong, leading to the bully's death, it becomes a war to see who will take over the social rankings of the school.

SYNOPSIS:

(Some characters' ages are not given).

At a high school, VERONICA SAWYER, 17, goes to find the Heathers. HEATHER MCNAMARA (17, black, shaved head, lesbian), HEATHER DUKE, 17, pale, male and identifies as gender-queer), and the Queen B, HEATHER CHANDLER (17, Fabulous, 245k followers). Heather Chandler does not like Veronica's outfit. Which means nobody likes Veronica's outfit.

But one outfit bothers Heather Chandler even more. RAM (jock) wears a jersey that some might find offensive to the Native Americans. Heather Chandler intimidates Ram to take off the shirt after she snaps a picture of him. As part of his penance, he must ask JESUS JULIE (17) if she'll do anal with him. Ram refuses, Heather threatens to post the photo on her socials and get him canceled, screwing his scholarship. He has no choice. Julie slaps him.

Bothered by it all. Veronica goes to the vending machine where JD (18, dark and mysterious), the new student, approaches her. He does not understand why she hangs out with the Heathers. Veronica seems interested in him.

Later, Veronica tells Heather Duke of JD, but their conversation is interrupted once they see Heather McNamara making out with a teacher, MR. WATERS, meaning Heather McNamara is just Black, not Black and gay. Now that's a betrayal. And with a teacher of all people? Gross... Duke takes a photo of it.

That night, Heather Chandler takes Veronica to a college party. Before they go inside, Heather asks Veronica to take a picture of her, but she is a jerk about the whole process. Leading to —

A DREAM SEQUENCE where Veronica buries Heather Chandler alive.

Later, Veronica sees Heather Chandler posted the picture of Ram with the jersey, after promising she wouldn't, so she confronts her. But Heather does not take crap from anybody, much less from Veronica. She intimidates her so much that Veronica takes a few steps back and bumps into a sculpture filled with a liquid. Tipping it. Breaking it. Exploding it and all the blue liquid inside. The whole thing splashes over Heather Chandler...

At first, Veronica is apologetic, but Heather is a jerk about it, so Veronica calls her a "fatty" in front of everyone. Heather is not too offended, after all, she can use this fat-shaming against Veronica.

Back home, writing in her diary, Veronica regrets what she said and wishes Heather would just die. JD surprises her, breaking in through the window. He wants to hang out. But once he reads her diary, he has an idea...

They go to Heather Chandler's house with a Nazi hat and some vomiting pills. The plan is to sneak in, put the hat on Heather's head, and snap a damaging and humiliating photo. And they do it. But before they can leave, Heather wakes up. JD tricks her into having a vomiting pill. But she does not vomit. She passes out. And dies. Only then he realizes he gave her the wrong pills. Veronica wants to call the police, but JD doesn't. Heather deserved this and they do not deserve the consequences. So instead, they fabricate Heather's suicide video and post it.

The next day, everyone in school is talking about it. The alive Heathers argue over who should be the one giving Heather Chandler's eulogy. Heather Duke ends up posting the photo of Heather McNamara to expose her for not being gay, winning himself the eulogy.

At the ceremony, Veronica is stressed whether people might know it's her fault. When the time comes for the eulogy, Heather Duke is ready to speak, but BETTY FINN (17, Asian, nerd) beats her to the podium. She gives a powerful speech about hate in high school and how all the students are one and the same. Everyone loves it and in a matter of seconds, Betty becomes popular. Will she become a jerk just like Heather Chandler?

CUT TO earlier that day when Heather Chandler's parents arrive home and see their daughter dead. But she is not dead. She vomits the pill and is all right. Then she checks her phone and understands what is happening. Sees "her own" suicide video and is not happy about it...

COMMENTS:

The show manages to skillfully talk about bullying and mental health amongst teenagers in a funny and self-aware manner. The script has very colorful characters, who all feel very realistic for a satire. The lead is strong and extremely empathetic. She truly is the embodiment of most teenagers, and her angsts are their angsts. There is a lot to like here, but a few minor things to be tweaked in order to make this a hit show.

The exposition is poorly delivered, with some dialogue that seems written simply to deliver information to an audience, on top of a diary, and dream sequences. Those lines need to be more skillfully integrated into the story, and the exposition needs to come more naturally or through conflict. On the other hand, the dialogue is strong in regard to the comedic genre. It is very quick and witty, with some gems that will be added to the audience's vocabulary.

Structurally, the script is simple, but works. A lot has been planted for future episodes, and a whole world is there. Nonetheless, the pilot moves at a fast pace with rising stakes, finishing up with a solid and unpredictable hook.

For the plot of the pilot, it would be beneficial to further focus on the lead character's relationship with other characters, instead of spending so much time on some seemingly less important secondary characters, like the teachers. This being because although, as mentioned, the pacing works, to further explore the lead might further cement the audience's engagement with the show, given how so much of the script is dedicated to plants for future episodes.

Another moment in the plot that needs restructuring is when JD shows up at Veronica's house and pushes for the whole revenge plan. It is a key moment in the story, but in the current version it seems forced into the story just because the plot point needs to happen, and it's not earned.

Characters-wise, the show's main antagonist, Heather Chandler is the most two-dimensional character in the pilot, with no indications of who she is and why, nor of what she wants. This seems to work in this short pilot and the audience needs to hate her, and given that she does not die, there is the opportunity to further develop her in future episodes. In contrast, the lead character is fully fleshed out, especially for a character that is supposed to be "ordinary." Her likability is high, and she is the perfect character to attract big talent.

The tone of this script seems in tune with the preferences for today's youth, and it does offer a lot of valid commentary on society. This series does require a network that is not afraid of some backlash, given that through humor it makes light of teenage suicide and has jokes about being fat, gay, and much more. Some members of the audience might not understand the liberal leaning politics of the show and misinterpret these as conservative attacks.

Overall, the project does have the added benefit of carrying the name of the cult classic movie, automatically having an audience of fans. On top of that, there are no shows out there with a similar tone, setting this one apart.

Comedic tone, realistic and engaging characters and a pilot that sets out a season to come, make this a strong project to be considered.

PROJECT: RECOMMEND

WRITER: CONSIDER

Exercises

Later, we'll write full coverage but for now, let's examine and practice some minor things.

1. What are at least three differences you notice between the different templates in this chapter?

2. Find a produced or unproduced script, then look at the second template which is for a large agency: Fill out everything up to and including short premise. Yes, there will probably be a lot of N/A's but get used to identifying the first few categories. Try your hand at it now, before the following chapters which cover things like loglines and synopses, to see how you do.

3. For the same script, write about one to two paragraphs of your comments. Again, we'll go over how to do this later on, but let's see how you start and compare it to your work by the end of the book. Like a nice "Before and After" comparison.

In summation, different companies ask for different categories and will each provide their own expectations and specifications. A lot of information will be provided, especially for the top parts where the coverage sets up the script. The biggest differences are between writing coverage for a writer, vs. for a boss or company that may be able to buy or sell it. Now that you have the context and templates for a quick overview, we can now explore each template category in greater detail.

Romance   Mystery   Drama   Action/Adventure

Comedy   Sci-Fi   Horror/Thriller   Family   Fantasy

3

Genre

Not So Easy, What About *Cowboys & Aliens* or *Black Panther*?

There are many genres out there and our first job as a Reader is to identify which one fits the script we are reading. It sets the mindset and mood for the person reading our coverage or hearing a pitch. For example, if I pitch a story about a father and son camping, it makes a difference if it's a family film, horror story, or a Muppet musical.

Think about how we choose to watch a movie or TV show. Often we base our decisions on the genre: "Do I feel like watching an art film, an adventure, or a period piece?"

That's why genre is the first element to consider when analyzing a screenplay. It is usually one of the first categories on the script coverage template — even above the logline. And there's a reason. Execs want to know the category (and some may even gauge their interest based solely on that) and they also need to know how to interpret the logline. Knowing the genre in advance helps buyers and sellers set expectations for a project so they can quickly decide if it's marketable and if it's what they want.

What Are Film Genres?

We all have our favorites genres or types of films, such as science fiction, comedy, or horror. Readers, agents, buyers, and audience members may discount or get excited about a script just from its genre. Some companies look for specific genres and reject others so a person submitting a script needs to do their diligence. For example, if we're reading for Seth Rogen's agent, they might not want *Littler Women* — a very serious period drama by Jane Austen's younger sister.

Readers are regular humans and as much as they want to be subjective, they have favorite genres and genres they don't like. Still, they must put those preferences aside and read them all. I love historical fiction but when I was a development executive at Juntobox, we were looking for low-budget independent films so we couldn't accept period pieces. And when I read for screenplay services and competitions, I might be more excited to read a period piece over a science fiction script but I always put my feelings aside and gave notes as suits the genre.

When a Reader gets a job writing coverage, it's important for them know what genres they like and what they don't. These preferences can affect their work if they don't learn to set them aside. Also, if they don't like superhero extravaganzas they shouldn't work for Marvel. If they don't like people returning to small towns from the big city and falling for the local bread maker they spurned in middle school, don't work for Hallmark, etc.

How Many Genres Are Out There?

There are lots of genres out there and more coming along all the time. Usually, the genre category is at the top of a coverage report, along with the word *form*, which asks whether it is a feature-length screenplay, a one-hour TV pilot, a half-hour pilot, a novel, etc. If the genre isn't clear, list the one or two genres that best fit.

Examples:

- *Us* directed by Jordan Peele, could be a horror or thriller.
- *Harry Potter & The Sorcerer's Stone* falls under fantasy fiction.
- *Atlanta* might be considered a half-hour dramedy, or an urban dramedy, or a comedy. It's not always clear.
- *American Horror Story* is a one-hour anthology series (a different story each season) and the genre is horror.

To determine genre, we must ask questions. Is the story based on action or a specific time period? Is it based on true events or not, or a location, such as the sea, in space, or on a battlefield? What gender, gender identity, race, or sexual preference does it examine? Do we see big explosions, sword fights, zombies, dragons, new lands, or old ones? And if there's a gang war, are the gangs in the inner city of Compton or 1920's Chicago? For science fiction, are we time traveling, falling in love with our own cell phone, or fighting on the planet Quargrar?

If we're laughing when reading a script — *are we supposed to be*? And are we laughing at farts, stoners, a love story, how many times Adam Sandler must prove he can be a grown-up, or the intrinsic nature of mankind?

Are people doing drugs and it's sad? Scary? Funny?

If we're scared is it by a monster (horror), a ghost (horror or supernatural), our *own mind* (psychological thriller), some fictitious blue-eyed thingy ghosts with swords that live beyond the Wall (period piece/ fantasy/action-adventure TV series)?

And now we have these amazing new genres that pop up — LGBTQ+, YA (Young Adult) dystopian, YA Dystopian... Oy. My parents enjoyed a nice western and adventure, usually proceeded by a newsreel.

If a big hero fights something big it's action. If someone goes somewhere and explores and fights, it could be adventure. If a normal person fights something that paralyzes them with fear — back to horror. And the beat goes on...

The Big Genres

Some of the top (most familiar or successful) genres are:

> **Drama** Usually more serious than humorous, like *12 Years A Slave* or the TV series *13 Reasons Why*. (No, dramas don't have to have numbers in the title.)
>
> **Comedy** Usually more humorous than serious (*The Big Sick* or the TV series *Insecure*).
>
> **Science Fiction** Dealing with any aspect of science that is not true or currently in our world. For example, writing about a character who has a cell phone isn't science *fiction*. We have those. However, a character who time travels, hops through other characters' minds or dimensions, or goes to other planets and galaxies is fiction (for now). (*Her* — a cellphone you fall in love with — or *Star Wars*.)
>
> **Romance** A story based on a love relationship (*A Star is Born* — any version — or *Portrait of a Lady on Fire*).
>
> **Action/Adventure** Usually in action, characters literally fight huge obstacles, antagonists, and elements. (*Kill Bill Vol. 1* and *The Dark Knight*). Adventure is usually when characters have a mission or quest and explore or travel to other locations. (*Lord of The Rings* or even *Stand By Me*.)

Horror/Thriller Horror usually involves some element/monster/thing that attacks from the outside (though it can get inside of people, physically like *Alien*, or spiritually as when someone is possessed.) **Thrillers** often have villains and attacks from the outside, but these focus more on suspense rather than blood, gore, or violence. For example, in a horror movie, Michael Meyers may jump out and try to kill people, whereas the film *Seven* makes us sit on the edge, not knowing where or when something creepy will happen. Many films are a combination of both. (Horror: *Halloween*. Thriller: *The Silence of The Lambs*).

Family Something kid-friendly that the whole family can watch, and a big genre for Disney and Pixar. (*Frozen* or *Marley & Me*).

Fantasy Like science fiction, it's fictitious, but it usually doesn't involve science or technology. It can have witches and wizards, magical elements or be set in a fictitious location or setting. This could range from fairy tales to *Game of Thrones* to *Harry Potter* to *Labyrinth*, etc.

Mystery Stories that focus on a puzzling crime, situation, or circumstance that needs to be solved, whether Agatha Christie's *Murder on the Orient Express* or Christopher McQuarrie's *The Usual Suspects*.

Try this Fun Exercise

Pretend you're coming up with an idea for a feature film and you write the following:

Someone battles something somewhere.

If you apply a different genre to this sentence and then add specifics, it gives you very different outcomes.

Examples:

Horror: Five Teenagers must fight a Man with a Hook at an Old Campground.

Whereas:

Romantic Comedy: An ex-nerd attends his high school reunion to finally go after his old crush — the ex-head cheerleader.

Family: A family adopts a bunny rabbit that multiplies faster than any before.

Western: A reluctant sheriff must rid their town of a vicious criminal posse.

The genres can dictate various type of worlds, characters, goals, obstacles and more.

Try applying the following genres to this intentionally vague idea:

> Two characters explore a new location.
>
> What would you write for:
>
> >A science fiction film?
> >
> >A comedy?
> >
> >A psychological thriller?
> >
> >A historical romance?
>
> Put in the specifics and see how different they are!

What About Sub-Genres?

Many genres include **sub-genres**. For example, comedy includes sub-genres like: broad comedy (*The Hangover*), buddy comedy, (*Superbad*) romantic comedy, *(When Harry Met Sally)* or dark comedy (the TV show *Succession*).

- Sub-genres of thriller includes psychological thrillers (*Get Out*), political thrillers, and spy movies.
- Action sub-genres include action-adventure (*Raiders of The Lost Ark*) and comedy-action *(Deadpool)*.
- Dramas have multiple subgenres including historical dramas (*Hidden Figures*), romantic dramas (*The Notebook*), coming-of age/young adult (*Hunger Games*).

And yes, sometimes we must put one before the other by figuring out which is dominant. For example, *The Godfather* is usually listed as a crime drama.

How Many Genres Should Be Attributed to a Script?

I believe listing one or two genres is good, but some scripts may border on three. If it seems like the script needs more than three genres, this might indicate a problem. For example, I might read a family comedy about a cute dog and then suddenly someone kills the dog and twenty more pages in sings about it, so: family/horror/musical?

However, consider a movie like *Black Panther*. It's superhero, but action, with science fiction elements. It also has adventure, drama, etc. It works and has quite a few genres.

Game of Thrones was a hit and could be considered action, adventure, drama, period, fantasy, etc.

Yet *Cowboys & Aliens* tried to combine different genres and it didn't quite work. Is it a western? Action? Sci-fi? Thriller?

Remember that genre is the category, and not just "the mood." For a time, Netflix listed odd categories as ads for their shows floated and rotated on the screen. They said things like "mindful", "intimate", "warm." These aren't genres. They convey the *tone*, which I will discuss in Chapter 12.

How Can I Figure Out What Genre This Confusing Script Is?

Sometimes a script has multiple genres.

Sometimes it works: *Back to The Future* – Adventure, comedy, sci fi.

Sometimes it doesn't: *Abraham Lincoln vs. Zombies* – Action, comedy, horror, period piece?

The key to the genre is usually contained in the:

> **Setting** (The future, WWII, the west, dystopia, civil war, Iraq, Compton).
> **Plot** (Guy must ask out 50 girls in 50 days, a killer is loose at a summer camp).
> **Character** (Jackie Robinson, the head of the Mafia, three African American women working at NASA).

And of course,

> **Subject matter** (A married man realizes he's gay.)
> **Tone** (Five stoned hot dogs forgot where they left the mustard and *hijinks ensue!*)
> **Brand** (It's owned by Marvel.)

Sometimes genre is obvious such as when the first few lines tell us we're in 1944 France and we immediately see a huge military battle. At other times we must infer as we read, but we'll all get better at that with practice.

And remember, there are lots of lists out there on the internet.

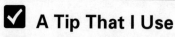 **A Tip That I Use**

Sometimes I'm reading (or writing) a script and I'm not exactly sure how I'd categorize it. So, I go to IMDB (the *Internet Movie Database*), look up similar films or shows to see how they are described. If you can't quite get the specific or dominant genre then take an educated guess. And educate yourself on different genres.

Exercises

1. List some genres. Try to list as many genres and subgenres as you can. Take some of the main genres I've mentioned and come up with subgenres. After that, see if you can name at least one movie or TV show that fits each genre in your list. For example: Family: Animated: *Encanto*.

2. Apply a genre to flesh out an idea: A logline is a one-sentence description of a script. In the next chapter we'll go over loglines in detail, but for now, I'm going to list a few loglines for some famous films. From these short descriptions, try to guess what genre or genres each movie might be. As a bonus, try to guess the title.

   • A mentally unstable Vietnam war veteran works as a night-time taxi driver in New York City where the decadence and sleaze he sees feeds his urge for violent action and leads him to attempt to save a preadolescent prostitute.

   • A quirky family determined to get their young daughter into the finals of a beauty pageant take a cross-country trip in their VW bus.

   • A seemingly indestructible android is sent from 2029 to 1984 to assassinate a waitress, whose unborn son will lead humanity in a war against the machines, while a soldier from that war is sent to protect her at all costs.

   • A seventeen-year-old aristocrat falls in love with a kind but poor artist aboard the luxurious, ill-fated *R.M.S. Titanic*.

   • When a killer shark unleashes chaos on a beach community, it's up to a local sheriff, a marine biologist, and an old seafarer to hunt the beast down.

   • A cowboy doll is profoundly threatened and jealous when a new spaceman figure supplants him as top toy in a boy's room.

   • A troubled child summons the courage to help a friendly alien escape Earth and return to his home world.

3. Using what you already know: What are some of the settings, traits, tropes, characters, or situations we might see in different genres?

   For example:

   Horror: Usually has a weak character (in older horror movies this was always a virgin, nowadays it's often teenagers) battling something or someone really huge. Horror stories often take place in remote or secluded places like a haunted house, the woods, or an abandoned summer camp. They often deal with battling fear.

   Young Adult/Coming of Age: Usually the characters are tweens (pre-teens), teenagers or college students, and these stories often deal with issues that occur between childhood and adulthood. These can be high school films and shows or even dystopian YA films like *Hunger Games*, that take place in a scary future. They often deal with the struggle of teens or young people growing up or gaining power.

Come up with some characters, themes, situations, and settings you might see in the following genres and subgenres:

Musicals	**Sports Drama**
War Films	**Detective Drama**
Superhero Movies	**Period Romance**

Who might the main characters be? Where and when might the story be set? What might be the characters' goals? Their obstacles? What else might they battle or struggle with (both externally and internally)?

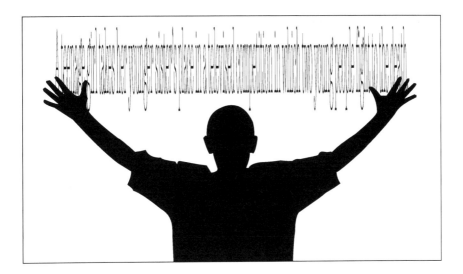

4

Loglines

Take their Opus and Squoosh It

Loglines are the bane of a writer's (and Reader's) existence. Why are they so important? Because sometimes that is the first and only shot a writer gets to pitch a project. Why are they so hard to write?

Because a writer crafted the *greatest dystopian four-hour epic that the world has ever seen! And graced it with musical numbers, 45 subplots, and an incredible backstory* and now they have to describe it in one sentence.

Writers write and there's a reason they aren't agents. They can't or don't want to market and sell their work themselves. Just because they can create amazing worlds, creatures, settings, and messages, doesn't mean they can package it into a great "must buy this right now" one-liner.

But writers need to know how to write great loglines. And so do Readers.

What Is a Logline?

A logline is a one- or two-sentence summary of a film that not only conveys the premise, but also gives emotional insight into the story as a whole.

A logline is often the first thing a buyer or representative wants to see. It's a first impression, and it can open or close the gates right there and then. In formal script coverage, the logline comes before the synopsis because it does not tell the whole story. However, it conveys the main character, goal, stakes, obstacle/antagonist, world, time period, and genre, and it must do this in one sentence. (It can be two but no more.)

Here's an example of a possible logline for the movie, *The Godfather*:

> The aging patriarch of an organized crime dynasty transfers control of his clandestine empire to his reluctant son.

And even this doesn't tell you the time period, cool subplots, secondary characters, specific antagonists, etc. That's because it can't convey everything and it shouldn't. But it needs to do one thing above all else:

> A logline doesn't TELL the story. It SELLS the story.

That is the objective of a logline — not to tell every precious detail but to garner interest from buyers and sellers.

What About Taglines?

There's a difference between a logline that sells a movie idea and what one might see on a movie poster, which is called a *tagline*. Movie posters often have a great image and a line to pique our interest. Sometimes they state a brand name, that the film is a sequel, or that it has huge stars.

The major difference between a logline and a tagline is that with a tagline the movie is already sold and made. It doesn't have to sell a concept and make people wonder if they should put time and money behind its development; that's already done. Word of mouth, trailers, ads, and other marketing elements have been added. In fact, a tagline is often not a full concept, just a tease.

Here's a tagline for the animated film, *Chicken Run*:

> She's poultry in motion.

It's cute, funny, and I've remembered it over the years, but I wouldn't open a pitch with that or list it as a logline because it's not specific. There's no context like we would find later when the movie has been released and we see the picture on the poster above the tagline. If I used that tagline from *Chicken Run* as a logline at the start of my coverage, my boss would have no idea what the movie is about.

On *IMBD.com* (*The Internet Movie Database*), *Chicken Run* is described as:

> When a cockerel apparently flies into a chicken farm, the chickens see him as an opportunity to escape their evil owners.

This might not be the actual logline but it's closer. And remember from Chapter 3, we would already have stated the genre (in this case, animated comedy) so a buyer would get a clear picture of the world, goal, stakes, and antagonist.

Here's tagline from *The 40 Year-Old Virgin*:

> The longer you wait, the harder it gets.

Fun, right? If we're in the know or see Steve Carrell's goofy face on the poster.

As opposed to (again IMDB's) logline:

> Goaded by his buddies, a nerdy guy who's never "done the deed" only finds the pressure mounting when he meets a single mother.

What Loglines Should Include

A great logline should tell us who is the main protagonist, the world or setting of the story (especially if it's fictitious, surreal, or special in some way), the goal of the main character(s), and set up the antagonist or obstacle. It should also be active and succinct.

Here's a bad example of a logline for the movie *E.T.*:

> An extra-terrestrial is stuck on earth and some kids discover him, but perhaps something about a boy finding an extra-terrestrial and helping it get home.

This logline is vague, doesn't include stakes and needs more about the protagonist, perhaps conveyed with an adjective.

Better example:

> A meek little boy must help a stranded extra-terrestrial get back to his planet.

But it still needs antagonistic forces.

> A meek little boy must help a stranded extra-terrestrial get back to his planet before the government discovers, kidnaps, and experiments on the gentle alien.

The more active, specific, and succinct, the better. We can also describe the antagonist a little too, like "evil government workers." We might include any stakes or time limits to convey tension.

Like this logline from the movie *Speed*:

> A young police officer must prevent a bomb from exploding aboard a city bus by keeping its speed above 50 mph.

The point is to identify the main character and tell what they *do*, not how they feel.

What Loglines Shouldn't Include

Feelings. Dialogue. Subplots (even if they are fantastic). Character names. Think about it. If I started the logline of *E.T.* as "Elliot must…" that doesn't tell us anything. Is he a boy? A man? A sponge? Names usually don't tell us anything *except*:

> **Whether the character is famous.** You can bet your Aunt Bippy it makes a difference to say, "Albert Einstein must eat an ice cream cone before it explodes…"
>
> **If the name tells us something.** This is rarer but if a logline began with "Virgin McScaredycat" decides to go on a road trip…"

If the name doesn't help paint a picture then we use adjectives. "Virginal," "alcoholic," "nosy" and so on.

The same goes for antagonists. I don't care that "Frieda must battle Owen" as much as "Batman battles The Joker…

Don't include settings if they don't matter, i.e. "An agoraphobic older lady *in the town of Slydell, Lousiana* never deals with the world outside her home…"

But if the world is crucial to understanding the concept then it needs to be mentioned, for example:

> A team of African American women must battle racism and sexism in 1960's NASA to not only hold onto their jobs but also help get the first man into space. — *Hidden Figures*.

> A paraplegic marine dispatched to the moon Pandora on a unique mission becomes torn between following his orders and protecting the world he feels is now his home. — *Avatar*.

> A teenage girl takes her younger sister's place in the Hunger Games - a televised competition in which two young people from each of the twelve districts of Panem are chosen at random to fight to the death. — *I'm not going to tell the title. Guess!*

Remember — don't tell the whole story, just get our interest. This also means: Don't tell us the ending. We don't need to know. Whether it's a writer pitching, or a Reader putting it on top of the coverage, the point is to *make 'em want to read it*. The exec will learn how it ends when they read the synopsis. Use the logline to make them want to find out.

How to Craft a Logline

Something I was taught to start out with at (shout out) UCLA film school was the following:

> A wants B but C is in the way, so they do D.

Basically, a protagonist has a goal but someone or something is in their way, so they take some very big action. This pretty much gets us to the end of Act One (we'll go into structure later).

If the set up or world is important, include it:

> In a world where children are grown in vats...

Or we may want to explain a world or major event...

> After a 100-year war that has left the earth without water... a poor orphan must...."

Remember to be succinct (practice composing tweets), use adjectives to convey the characters, and active verbs (*decimate* is so much more interesting than *deliberate*).

And the Concept?

The logline conveys the idea or *concept* and oftentimes that's what a buyer or seller is interested in. What is the script about, has it been done before, and if so, was it done successfully? For example, if an agent reads the full logline of *E.T.* written above, they can figure out if it's a fresh concept (little kids help a cute alien go home) and if they can picture it and/or make money from it.

An agent or exec might think, "Ok. Cute kids, cute alien. Big stakes, evil antagonists, pulls the heart strings... Yeah I can see it." (Or even more important ("Yeah, I can sell it.") But do they always want a new concept? One that has never been done before? (An army colonizes Mars?) Or the true and tired concept (a half-hour sitcom about a funny guy and his wife and kids)? Let's explore.

Hollywood loves the term "familiar yet different" because they can base their thinking on a previous project that has been successful (familiar) but with an additional unique (different) something that suggests the film will be a big hit. There's a common trope in pitching a concept where people state, "It's like X meets Y."

For example, *The Big Bang Theory*:

> *Friends* meets *Revenge of the Nerds*.

You can picture it and compare it to two other successful projects.

Or the movie I've always dreamed of:

> *Jurassic Park* meets *Yentl* = *Hassidic Park*.

Some people like describing scripts in this mash-up way because it can give an immediate context, while others find it a bit derivative.

We can also refer to a successful movie or genre and give it a twist. Such as many action-movie pitches where they might say, "It's *Die Hard* but, in a child's bouncy house." Or pitching the original *Star Trek* as "A western in space."

These are examples of *high-concept* projects where the idea can be conveyed in a line or two. There are also perfectly wonderful *low-concept* ideas, which I'll get into in a moment.

The logline should convey the concept, but some companies also want Readers to rate or comment on the concept and provide a section for that in their coverage template. They ask the Reader if the script has a high-concept or low one, is it marketable, timely, does it have an audience, etc.?

What Makes an Idea High- or Low-Concept?

High-concept films and shows can be pitched or understood simply and easily. The idea is a big part of the hook and executives can get it in a few sentences. Many blockbusters are like this.

Examples:

> ***Liar, Liar:*** A lawyer who built his entire career on lying, finds himself cursed to speak only the truth for a single day, during which he struggles to maintain his career and to reconcile with his ex-wife and son whom he alienated with his pathological lying.
>
> ***Groundhog Day:*** A cynical television weatherman covering the annual Groundhog Day event in Punxsutawney, Pennsylvania becomes trapped in a time loop forcing him to relive February 2nd repeatedly.
>
> ***Freaky Friday:*** A mother and her daughter switch their bodies and get a taste of each other's lives.
>
> ***Spy Kids:*** Real spies, only smaller.
>
> ***Snakes on a Plane:*** Seriously. I don't have to say anything else.

They say *Twins* was pitched as: "Danny Devito. Arnold Schwarzenegger. Twins.

And of course, nowadays, we can also pitch a concept that might not be high, just familiar, like sequels and reboots such as *Spiderman Yet Again…* or *Avengers XVIII — The Musical*.

High-concept movies often have unique worlds like *Waterworld* and *Westworld* but perhaps not *Wayne's World* (a smaller movie, but the characters were already known.)

Low-concept movies put less of a focus on the concept, brand, or big plot, and more on characters, relationships, or themes within the plot itself.

They can be harder to pitch and are often dependent on the execution.

Consider a movie like *Juno*:

> Faced with an unplanned pregnancy, an offbeat young woman makes an unusual decision regarding her unborn child.

Not the most original concept or premise, but a very enjoyable film because of the writing, characters and acting. Many independent films fall into this category.

While many agents, production companies, and networks believe it's easier to sell a high-concept project, they may also want projects with high-quality or emotionally moving writing, something lower-budget, a role an actor can sink their teeth in or garner Oscar buzz, etc. In this case the Reader must convey that while the concept may not be big, the script has a lot of intrinsic worth.

In some competitions or companies, we are asked to rate how good the concept is, which can be a little difficult. If there is a category (such as in the alternate competition template in the Appendix at the back of the book) asking to give a score to the concept, but it's a low-concept project, I might rate it low but also note that it is not intended as a high-concept movie and extol any other attributes.

We must consider our own preferences. Sometimes we might feel like watching superheroes save the planet and other times we want to see the moving story of an immigrant family's journey towards a better life. And while it seems like high-concept means more expensive and a chance to make more money, that's not always the case. Which brings us to the question…

Why Are Daddy and Santa Claus Never in the Same Room at the Same Time?

Sorry, wrong book.

Can Something Be Both High-Concept and Low-Budget or Vice Versa?

Often futuristic, superhero, historical dramas, huge war films, and so on, mean bigger budgets, but not always. This is where we remind ourselves that high-concept might not be the best term since it evokes thoughts of high budgets, but it's the term we've got right now.

A good example is *Room:*

> Held captive for seven years in an enclosed space, a woman and her young son finally gain their freedom, allowing the boy to experience the outside world for the first time.

This feels low-budget and like it will rely on characters, relationships, and internal struggles but the concept is easy to picture. Many horror movies fall into this category.

High-concept/low-budget seems happen more often than low-concept/high-budget. Obviously, some low-concept movies can have a higher budget once A-list talent comes on board, and it doesn't take a high concept to think of the 45th *Fast and The Furious* movie, but that isn't what I'm talking about. Low-concept/high-budget is usually more about the execution as opposed to the concept. One example could be *Out of Africa:*

> In 20th-century colonial Kenya, a Danish baroness/plantation owner has a passionate love affair with a free-spirited big-game hunter.

The world is intriguing and there are some conceptual hooks but it's basically a place, a love story and two big name actors of the time, Robert Redford, and Meryl Streep.

Or perhaps *Ocean's Eleven:*

> Danny Ocean and his ten accomplices plan to rob three Las Vegas casinos simultaneously.

Concept-wise, three simultaneous robberies is original, but the movie is mostly about getting a team together and pulling a heist using a lot of A-list actors.

And similarly, *Knives Out* has a huge cast and lots of twists and surprises, but its concept?

> A detective investigates the death of a patriarch of
> an eccentric, combative family.

Most road trip movies (where people go somewhere and it's really about their character arcs and experiences) are low-concept, but where they go and what happens along the way can affect the budget.

The bottom line is that high-concept projects can be pitched and pictured succinctly and easily, while low-concept ones are usually more thought-provoking, internal, or about the people and their journeys. The former is easier to pitch, and the latter may be better to read for oneself. A Reader can also state how well a concept is executed, or, in the case of a low-concept project, how great the story, characters, and content are.

Premise or Concept?

For most companies, when they say *premise,* they mean *concept.* That is, "What is the idea?"

One exception when premise *does not mean* concept occurred when I read for two different agencies. They each had a category on their coverage template labeled "premise" which meant that we had to give an additional and shorter summary.

Go to the templates and look at the agency examples. They ask for a logline (1-2 sentences) and a synopsis (which I'll go over in the next chapter — anywhere from 1-4 pages), and then in between that is a one or two paragraph summary which they call "premise." These examples are the exception, and I'm not sure why they need a premise. Perhaps the agents read that first and decide if they should ignore this project or go on and read the longer synopsis, but I don't believe that. I think agents go on anyway because they know what they're looking for and need the synopsis.

So, to recap (and each company will clarify their definition) for the most part the "premise" category means concept — and on some occasions it means a shorter synopsis.

How Do You Craft a Logline When You Can't Figure Out What the Script Is About?

All Readers will encounter this: we read the big, meandering, aquatic, space opera and now have to write coverage for it. It may be well-written, but the plot isn't easy to convey or isn't clear, yet we're still expected to convey the plot clearly.

In the UCLA MFA Screenwriting program we had a joke about pitching projects wherein we'd just add "and hijinks ensue" to kind of suggest we had no idea where our comedy was going but we hoped it would be funny. However, if we write that as the logline, it indicates an issue.

It's hard to cover a script where the main plot isn't clear — or maybe there are competing plots and subplots and it's hard to discern which is the main one. That's why in my younger days, I (cringe) turned out some of the following gems:

> A farmer does all he can to save his farm, battling progress, the times, and his brother's desire to sell it.

> When a man is found dead, we go back two months and learn interweaving stories of drug deals, cheating, and desperation that led to it.

> Four women, fed up with partners or single status, move in together with their kids and establish a friendly, supportive new community.

Scripts can meander, be unclear, or unfocussed. However, both writers and Readers must do the best they can to convey a concept and logline succinctly and actively.

Exercises

1. A good start to crafting a logline:

This is something I did in film school as a student and now teach my students. For my coverage students, this teaches them to craft a logline with the essential parts. For my writing students, it's a good way to brainstorm, since it forces one to think actively.

Think of it as a logline formula:

> A (protagonist) wants B (goal) but C (obstacle/antagonist) is in the way so they D (take an action)

Use specifics to include stakes and more. For example:

> A blind boy wants to roller-skate but his parents won't let him, so he hitches his skates to a seeing eye dog and enters the national roller-skating derby.

Try a few. And once you have a basic one, look at how to make the conflict bigger. Or the stakes higher.

For example, a boy wants to date a girl... is vague, but: In 1969 Ireland a Protestant boy wants to date a Catholic girl... Specific. Put the cat up a tree, throw rocks at it, and then set it on fire.

And when you've done this, you can then go back and play with genre. If you change it to a horror project, could the boy be a ghost?

Have fun and play.

2. High or low concept?

You decide:

- Follows the lives of eight very different couples in dealing with their love lives in various loosely interrelated tales all set during a frantic month before Christmas in London, England — *Love, Actually*
- A group of intergalactic criminals must pull together to stop a fanatical warrior with plans to purge the universe — *Guardians of the Galaxy*
- A faded television actor and his stunt double strive to achieve fame and success in the film industry during the final years of Hollywood's Golden Age in 1969 Los Angeles — *Once Upon a Time in Hollywood*
- In England in 1987, a teenager from an Asian family learns to live his life, understand his family, and find his own voice through the music of Bruce Springsteen — *Blinded by the Light*
- A disillusioned college graduate finds himself torn between his older lover and her daughter — *The Graduate*

3. Come up with a high-concept and a low-concept idea. For fun. They can be "bad".

Here are my lovely concoctions (that I will never write):

- A fleet of two million genetically modified space ducks must save 85 galaxies in two hours.
- A man goes for a walk.

And I can change the budget by adding to the first one "in a sketch on paper," or for the second — "Off the plank and then challenges pirates using all the Greek gods and a lot of special effects!"

5

Synopses

Just the Facts, Ma'am

How to Craft a Synopsis

We've all done this before: we've summarized plots *and often given spoilers* to our loved ones. Or we've had to recount stories and, afterwards, realized we hadn't given enough detail:

```
              SEINFELD
    We went to the bedroom and then
    yada yada yada… she was dead the
    next morning.
```

So, Goldilocks, if this one is too short and this one is too long, what's a happy medium? It depends on who we're writing for. Most competitions or script services that provide coverage for *writers* ask for a *brief* synopsis or summary or perhaps none at all since the writer already knows their own story. However, most agents, buyers, sellers, and executives ask for longer synopses because they don't know the story and need the Reader to relay it to them.

Basically, a *synopsis* is a recounting of the main points of the story, and it takes a bit of finesse to weave in some tone and themes or hooks — so writing a synopsis is not for the faint of heart —but it can be done.

The synopsis is usually presented before comments so that our boss can learn what the script is about, and then see how well it was written. In most coverage templates, we will be told how long the synopsis should be.

Example: Synopsis of a Feature Script

(Some of the characters' ages weren't given.)

1947. Arizona. The Short Creek Raid forces Mormon Fundamentalists to run, scatter, denounce their religion and polygamous ways, and sends JOHN HANCOCK, his pregnant wife EDITH, and daughters, JEANNIE, EDDA, and LISA into the desert. After building a makeshift home and dealing with malnutrition and dehydration, John dies, just as his youngest daughter, KAZIAH MAY is born. As her mother is too dehydrated to nurse her, Kaziah May's older brother, ROD, nurses her from a goat and takes them to Utah where other Fundamentalists have settled.

1955. 7-year-old Kaziah (now called May), a budding young artist is close to her rebellious brother until BARD and NANAS KANDERHOSH come around with food and aid for the family and fill young May's head with visions of God and the teachings of Fundamentalism. WALT, an elderly man, and a boarder in Edith's house, also aids in the children's education by taking them to meetings. May enjoys these meetings and the feelings they instill in her. She especially loves listening to the ebullient preacher, BROTHER MARVIN, and his depictions of Heaven and "our Father who Art in it." May dreams of her father and wants very much to get to heaven and be reunited with him. She begins to take her religion seriously.

When May is fifteen, and as Jeannie, the last of her sisters, gets married and leaves, Walt proposes to May. She is appalled and Bard says he will speak to Brother Marvin about whom she is supposed to marry. Shocked, he returns and tells May that she is meant for him - Bard. May objects but when Walt and Bard put her brother Rod in a mental institution for not obeying and following The Principles, she acquiesces. Plus, according to Fundamentalist law, May's parents' marriage was never properly sealed in the eyes of God. Bard tells May that he is the only way she has of going to heaven and possibly saving her mother's soul.

At age 15, May enters Bard's house and becomes his third wife.

May is repulsed at the condition of Bard and Nanas' house and quickly instructed in the hierarchy (she is the lowest) in the family. Nanas is the highest and the house mother; ZOSA, a cockeyed outspoken woman cleans and will have the babies; and May will work the bottle cleaning business with Nanas' nephew, WILL. She will also service Bard whenever he wants, which is all the time. Zosa is jealous but May doesn't know why. She hates servicing Bard. She loses herself in her work and her faith.

May's art is squelched but she channels her talents into the business. Over time she invents and creates many inventions and labor-saving devices. She designs and builds large machines and transforms the business into a larger moneymaker. JOSEPH MANLEY, a Mormon (non-Fundamentalist) who works at the hardware store and is amazed at this little woman's drive and talent, assists her. He helps her out of kindness and perhaps a little more. The more they work, the more May gets a taste of the kindness that is out there that she has been missing. She also gets a taste of love.

As Joseph shows May her worth, she comes to the family with a few demands. One is to help her mother. Bard brings Edith in to live but gets her to sign away her property to him. Now she is enslaved in the house. She is beaten and treated like dirt. Bard constantly reminds her that her marriage to her husband was not sealed, and she is going to Hell. When May tries to intervene, Bard threatens Edith's life.

In time, Will brings home a wife, THERESA, who becomes May's friend and a good example. She doesn't put up with half of the things May and Zosa put up with. As Zosa gets pregnant and realizes May doesn't want Bard like she does, they too become friends. The women all help Zosa deliver her babies, year after year. And year after year the babies are taken from Zosa and given to Nanas to raise as Bard tells Zosa she's too filthy and stupid to raise her own children. Everything in the house belongs to all. May is forbidden to get pregnant because she must work the business and stay sexy for Bard. When Theresa has a child, she refuses to give him up to Bard and Nanas, as it didn't come from either of them.

As May and Joseph build larger machines for the business, the two care for each other too deeply. Joseph is married and isn't a polygamist. He is amazed to discover that May is. They wish they could be together. Joseph tells her how much more she deserves —someone even better than him. She starts to see that she deserves more and asks Bard for a deed to the business. If it isn't in his name, he can qualify for more Welfare. He likes this idea but he signs the business over to Will. May goes on strike, her customers support her, and Will, who can't manage it at all, finally says he's giving the business back to May. During this strike, Bard takes his anger out on Edith. May runs to Brother Marvin to get them out of this situation, but he and Bard put her in the mental institution to scare her back into submission. There she sees Rod, mellow and castrated (literally) and freaks. Bard appears (her "savior") and checks her out of there. When she gets home, he threatens her mother's life if May ever tries to escape again. May sees that her mother is getting sicker and comes up with a plan.

All this time, May's sisters, Edda and Lisa were both married and kept at home so no one would know that their husbands had many wives. No one knows where Jeannie is. Finally, they hear from her, and May's plan goes into action. She gets Edith to a hospital where they are reunited with Jeannie who works as a nurse. Jeannie is widowed (so she is free) and will take her. Joseph drives Edith to Jeannie's house (where she will also get Rod out of the institution) and May plans her escape.

The next morning, after instructing the workers, and telling Joseph she loves him but must belong to herself now, she packs up to go. Bard catches her but her workers help restrain him. Theresa has taught her how to drive and she takes off — away from her imprisonment and off to freedom. Her own woman.

Who Wants Them and What Are They Used For?

Synopses are more important to buyers and sellers than they are to writers. However, some competitions and coverage services provide in-depth synopses, which may be helpful to the writer. Often, as a writer, I have pitched a project to my agent or a production company and then been asked for a synopsis, so it's nice to have one written by an objective eye. Many writers have a hard time knowing what to include and what to omit. "Audiences must know everything! No detail left behind! They're all sooooo important!!!"

So, if we're writing coverage for a writer, a synopsis may help them when they try to sell the project.

When writing coverage for an exec, as their gatekeeper or *the first to read the script,* synopses are very important. When presented with a big stack of scripts, our job is to find the diamond in the rough. We say "gatekeeper" because the Reader is the first line of defense. If they recommend a script, it goes through to the next level.

When writing a synopsis that will be read by an exec, remember:

1. **It's the Reader's job to make their boss's job easier.** Agents and execs get countless scripts and can't possibly read them all. Readers are there to summarize the story and then explain them how well the story was executed.

2. **Most likely the exec has not read the script, so they rely on the Reader to be their eyes.** Our job is to relay the story to them so the exec or agent can understand it. Depending on a Reader's recommendations (and sometimes despite their recommendations), the exec will decide if they should read the script themselves. The synopsis must convey the plot, while being

thorough, and engaging. We must figure out how to emotionally invest the exec in the story because that's what scripts, films, TV shows and so on need to do. Whether the story is scary, dramatic, big budget sci-fi, or romantic-comedy, people buy and make film projects to engage people. So, we must use our talents to summarize the plot and convey it to someone who's never read it. Rather than just regurgitating the main points, we must take them on a journey.

Telling the Story

A screenplay needs to have momentum — it must continually move forward. A synopsis must have momentum as well, and it must achieve it even more efficiently than the original script.

For the most part, in a synopsis we're relating the main plot points. We won't include that wonderful funny line that Lamar says to Ralph about how his elbow smells, even though it may be the most memorable part of the movie. (We can save the kudos to the dialogue for our comments later on.)

We also won't always include all the deep themes and messages, such as how Ralph cared more about saving the polar ice cap than washing his elbow — and in the end shouldn't we all? Again, we can mention those things in the comments section, or find a way to show them in the synopsis.

For example:

> With T-5 minutes, Ralph sniffs his elbow, turns away, and smashes it into the villain's face. He then jumps in the icy water and saves the drowning polar ice cap, leaving the island with drinking water for generations!

We can also include important subplots if we pull it off as economically as possible.

All that said, writing a synopsis is hard work. Don't be surprised if we encounter these two problems:

- **What if the plot is confusing and I can barely follow it and it's not my fault, it's the writer?**
  We must drop the blame and do our best. Hopefully, if later in the comments we state this as an issue, our boss will understand.

- **What if the script has a million time jumps and flashbacks, or is set in multiple time periods?**
  Ditto. We do our best. There are some tricks I employ, such as putting the time periods in bold — this is like introducing new

characters in capitals. It draws the eye to new and different situations and keeps track of things.

For example:

```
EXT. LIVING ROOM - PRESENT DAY

MARK, 6, sits next to BOOPSIE, 6, acting
nonchalant, then runs out of the room. He
has an asthma attack and the corridors of
the elementary school swirl.

IRAQ, 2019: Mark, now 4, is on the front
lines with Boopsie's photo on his sleeve…
```

Remember that our main job is to clearly convey a story that our boss has never read. And since synopses can go on for a couple of pages, we can keep track of people, places, and things. Or as I call them —nouns.

Another thing to notice in the above example is that if we see the same character during another time period after introducing them, we can state their age in that sequence, but don't need to put their name in capitals. I first introduced Mark in the present, and put his name in capitals, along with his age. But when I flashed back to 2019 Mark didn't need to be capitalized, since we already met him, but I give the age he is now.

If a script jumps back and forth in time a lot, or if we feel the need to synopsize scenes out of order, then do. The answer to how to organize a synopsis always comes down to the question, "What is the best way to relay the story so that someone else gets it?"

Or, to put it another way: *relay* the story in a way that the boss can *picture* it. That's why I don't say we're telling a story. We are relaying it.

What to Include and What to Exclude

When writing a synopsis, Readers have to decipher which main points are important. Even if these points are unclear in the script, we'll need to relay them in the best way possible. However, keep in mind it's not an exact science. We have to make decisions on a per-script basis. For example, some high-concept scripts can be summarized easily:

```
They go to this island, battle pirates, save the
princess…
```

Whereas a low-concept story relies more on the execution.

```
BENNY, 26, hates his job at the toxic nuclear
sneaker shop and longs to get out of town. His
parents have carved a niche among the town's
sneaker-industrial elite and put a lot of pressure on
```

> him, as he's the last in the line, due to his mother's
> previous children having been born blobby and with
> too many eyes.

Sometimes it's the tiny details that are important, so include them if they're needed. If we're ever confused about what to include, always remember this: As the only one who has read the script, and as our boss' eyes and ears — what needs to be known?

Our job in the synopsis is to engage the boss in the story, as best we can, whether or not we believe they should buy, sell, or represent the script. Later, there will be a chance to say if we think they should do any of those things. In the meantime, let them go through the journey themselves, because sometimes they may see something we don't. For example, maybe a script's plot isn't that great, but an agent has an A-list action director dying to do a fish romance — and this one happens to have one!

Keep Your Opinion to Yourself

The synopsis is objective — it relates only the facts. Tell the boss what happens in a way they can see and feel it.

A synopsis is not subjective, and yet it's also not as dry or cold as a newspaper article. A synopsis tells the story, leaving out opinion. The tone of the synopsis, while professional, should skew towards the tone of the script. We can convey the excitement of the action or the depths of a betrayal in our word choices.

For example, as opposed to just writing:

> The pirate fights and wins.

We can write:

> The pirate king cuts down a growing number of
> escalating assassins while the ship careens toward
> a polar ice cap!!!!!

In this way I can convey the suspense and tension, while still only relaying the major plot points.

And instead of blandly summarizing:

> Bethany's mother didn't show up.

We could WRITE:

> After promising four times, Bethany's mother didn't
> show up to help her with prom.

That shows a sadder picture. It also helps immerse the boss in the story, rather than just reporting it in a dry manner.

And when I say be objective, that means we have to watch our tone. I'll get into that more in Chapter 17. But as an example, I might not like the script, but I should never show that in the synopsis. For example:

> After promising four times, Bethany's lame mother didn't show up to help her with her weirdo prom.

Finally, watch out for tiny things like being overenthusiastic or under-enthusiastic and pushing an agenda (for the umpteenth time- that's what the comments section is for, and even then, we use caution). Be clear, be simple, be cohesive, be vivid. And be objective.

Additional Do's and Don'ts

- **Synopses should be in the present tense** (except for flashbacks or a few backstory explanations) so it feels like it's unfolding and can grab the Reader better. Ex: "Peter goes to the lab" as opposed to "Peter went to the lab."

- **Capitalize main characters and give their ages** when they're first introduced. That part is like writing a screenplay. This way if the boss reading the coverage gets lost, they can scan back to where the character was first introduced and get back on track. Knowing the ages of characters is important for casting, marketing, and envisioning. For example, if we write "MARK is determined to get his ex-girlfriend back" and omit that Mark is six, we lose quite a bit of context. So… "MARK, 6, enters his first day of first grade and there he sees her - BOOPSIE, 6, the one who broke his heart at the kindergarten formal last year when she dumped him for "L'il Craig."Notice I don't put characters in capitals or give their age if we just hear about them as opposed to meet them. If Li'l Craig makes an actual appearance then we cap that kid!

- **Break up long passages** to frame important information so that it doesn't overwhelm or bog down anyone's mind. White spaces help things flow, help important information get noticed and framed, and provide a user-friendly experience. However, it's not an exact science so don't go crazy with it. Take into consideration the length required by the company that hired us. If they want a one- to two-page synopsis and we have a lot to convey, we'll do what we have to do. Ditto if we need to stretch out a simple tale over four pages. Also, I write my synopses, (and my comments) in essay form. Again, breaking up information and paragraphs is easier on the eye and easier for the brain to follow.

- **Skip lines between paragraphs and don't indent.** I never heard anything said one way or another, but when I see my students' doing both, it feels a bit much.

Why I Didn't Impress Tim Allen's Company with My 14-Page Coverage

When writing a synopsis, we often must convey complicated ideas but above all we're shortening the story. So, folks, don't do what I did…

When I was just a newbie, I had an opportunity to interview as a Reader for Tim Allen's Boxing Cat Films. Well, I wanted to impress. And show off all I knew. So, I turned in a 14-page coverage … and never heard back.

I did not know the ginormous rule I've been conveying about how we're there to make an employer's jobs easier. Mathematically speaking, if they got 1000 scripts and a Reader gives them 5-pages per coverage — that's 5000 pages to read. But if they'd hired me, they'd have to read 14 page-documents on all 1000, or 14,000 pages.

Nope. Didn't get the job. Learned a lesson, got other jobs, never got to put on boxing gloves with a feline. But learn from my mistake: less is more.

The synopsis is the only purely objective part of written coverage. As we move on to the comments, which is a larger part of this book, I'll go over how to give our opinions, but even those need to be reined in to appear objective and professional.

So, my synopsis on this whole chapter? Keep it clear, simple, and easy to read. Save them time. That's what matters.

Exercises

1. Read this short synopsis and then answer the questions underneath:

NANCY, 40s, is a painter and art teacher married to BART, 48, whose company isn't doing well. Nancy is diagnosed with MS, and seems to not be able to paint, yet needs to in order to make money. Bart leaves her, she starts deteriorating, is put on leave, and tries to mentor a troubled girl and teenage mother, LINDA. Nancy meets LARRY, 35, at an MS support group, and the two have a romance. However, Nancy's frustrations lead her to break it off with him, insult Linda, and even when she switches to abstract art, she can't appease a potential buyer. She apologizes to Larry, but he doesn't forgive her, and then — after she has gotten a new apartment, sold some of her new work, helped Linda get into a university, and may work as an art consultant — the two reconnect and decide to enjoy their life down to the last drop.

- What is clear?
- What isn't? What questions do you still have?
- What do you think the genre is?
- Does it sound like something an agent or development executive might be interested in or not? Why?

Note how we get the gist, but may want details, and also we have no idea how well written it is. That's why the comments are so important.

2. Do a 1-½ page synopsis of a (not too popular) screenplay.

While you could watch a film and summarize it, since we're learning how to do coverage on scripts, it's best to practice on those. Remember to introduce all new characters in capitals and give their ages (if given). If not, you might write, CHARACTER, (age N/A). Decide which are the crucial points someone would need to know and write those in a clear, succinct and engaging way. To get the most out of this exercise, I suggest writing a synopsis of a film that's not that popular or well-known, then give the synopsis to a friend who has never seen or read the original. They will be reading it "blind", just as a future employer might. See if it's clear. What questions do they have?

3. Try a shorter synopsis.

Do a one paragraph version of the longer synopsis you wrote for the previous exercise. Can you shrink it to its most essential components? Not only do competitions and coverage services need short summaries, but there are some execs and companies that also want very short summaries and a few even want a certain word count, which is rare but it does happen.

6

Character

People to Read and People to Cast

To be able to evaluate the characters in a script, Readers need to understand what it takes to create a good one. Let's look at how to write, assess, and even help writers improve the characters in a screenplay.

I Know What They Are, But What Do I Look For?

My father was a real character. He was colorful, loud, had a strong opinion, good sense of humor, and a foul mouth. You can understand this, intellectually, but it's better if I paint you a picture of Bert Neufeld. I used to describe him as, "Woody Allen with the mouth of a NY cab driver." Since opinions have changed towards Woody Allen, I now say he was like Larry David — but less whiny.

But what if I could *show* who he was with an example? Like how I (true story) won a competition for a *Curb Your Enthusiasm* spec script, based on things my father actually did: in his 60's, this N.Y. Jewish man got kicked out of an art class for fighting with the nude model. When I wrote another script based on my childhood, his first line came so easily: "Pass me the cereal that helps me crap." Does this give a bit of a picture of my father?

Characters are the people or animals in films, shows, games, etc. They are the heart and soul of any story. They are the reason *why* we care. In my screenplay outlining classes, we may discuss how the story will go, but it ain't gonna fly if the main character isn't driving it.

While high-concept movie genres like sci-fi, horror, or action seem to focus on a world, a particular threat, or a quest, audiences need to emotionally invest in the characters and their journeys before any of those things will matter. To emotionally connect to a high-concept idea, we must put ourselves into a character's shoes.

And although much gets added once the project is cast, shot, and edited, we still need to start with clear and intriguing characters written on the page for two reasons:

1.   Whoever reads the script must become engaged and find a point of emotional investment. They need to identify, sympathize, root for, or connect to the characters to become interested in the story.
2.   Buyers/sellers, talent, and casting people need to see how the characters and roles could attract A-list talent, which makes a project more marketable.

So, whether we're writing or criticizing a script, let's examine what makes a strong character.

Are They Distinctive?

Heath Ledger as the Joker. Joaquin Phoenix as the Joker. Even Cesar Romero as the Joker. Basically, the Joker is a memorable character. In some of the different films that contain the Joker, we see that he believes that Batman has ruined his face and his life. In others he deals with some sort of mental illness. He is dangerous, unpredictable, smart, and back in the 1960's had a flair for tying heroes to pieces of wood and feeding them very slowly to a woodchipper. Whatever his motives and methods were, he was interesting.

We want our characters to be interesting and what's more...Hollywood likes characters that are *familiar yet different*.

Allison Reynolds (Ally Sheedy) in *The Breakfast Club*. Dustin in *Stranger Things,* Pray Tell in *Pose*, Tyrion Lannister in *Game of Thrones*, Minny Jackson in *The Help* (think "pie scene"), Olivia Pope in *Scandal*, Michael Corleone in *The Godfather,* etc.

Although actors add a lot, these roles started out distinctive on the page.

Distinctive characters don't have to be created from scratch. We may have seen them before. Cinema is over one hundred years old and plays, books, and stories are even older. I'm sure back in the time of ancient Rome, they sat around and peeled each other grapes and as someone recounted a recent battle, a "critic" rolled his eyes and thought, "Always with the marching and the killing and the formations. Can we get a romance where Greeks travel to Rome for a romantic vacation and call it *Roman Holiday*? Or can a soldier be dissatisfied with fighting and dream of making it in musical theater instead? I'm sick of the same ol' Coliseum Cinema."

In the animated film *101 Dalmations,* Cruella de Vil wanted to kill puppies, make them into coats, and move on. However, the same character in another movie, *Cruella,* was much more complex. She had psychological issues, strengths, and flaws.

Give 'em a twist and characters can become more interesting.

Beyond Stereotypes

There can be a sense of freedom in inventing a character and putting our own spin on them. There will always be the non-popular kid, the cop about to retire, the person in the dead-end town who wishes they could escape, the outsider, the unrequited lover, the killer, or the hero. How do we make those characters distinctive?

Notice I didn't say "different" because some people might think they have to make the person something we've never seen and probably don't want to, or they'll simply change one tiny thing, like "a cop who wants to retire in *two* months instead of just one".

Distinctive characters don't arise from thinking of something tiny to add (like a mole on their cheek). Characters are different because of who they are, what they want, and what actions they take. What are their dreams, flaws, and circumstances? And why should we care about them? To find an interesting character we must start from the inside.

The character of a regular sea monster might not be so easy to write because it's a cliché or a mythical being, but with a clear POV it could be: "The sea monster that wants to be understood." Now it's got a conflict, a goal, and struggles. I can develop it even further: "It's little, its roar is small, it's being trained to be scary but wants to befriend a fisherman's young son…" Now I can make $$$$ for Disney+.

It's Who You Know

Another good way to create a distinctive character is to base them on someone you know. Years ago, when people wanted to become staff writers on TV shows, they often wrote a sample episode of a different but similar series to show their ability to capture the voices of a show's main characters. (It had to be another series for legal reasons. For example, when I wanted to get a job writing on *Will & Grace*, I wrote a *Friends'* sample script as well as a *Seinfeld* sample.)

Seinfeld characters were easy for me to capture. I could totally predict how George Costanza from *Seinfeld* would react in any situation. I put him in a co-dependents' anonymous meeting where he said he was an alcoholic in order to meet women. It seemed like something he'd do.

In other scripts, I've written about people I know. I might write something very autobiographical and write the characters as they are in real life, or in other cases I might use some aspect of a real person but fictionalize it. The characteristics are already known to me. For example, when I write characters based on my father, I know that he would want a cereal that makes him crap, argue with nude models, etc.

However, when we write about people we know, we must get beyond our opinion of them and let them be three-dimensional. For example, if my mother was mean (she wasn't) and I write her as such, I'll get about a minute of catharsis and then be left with a one-dimensional character. Can I get into her head and heart and convey what her fears, goals, dreams, and arcs would be? I'd have to.

Therefore, when writers base characters on people they know, Readers must make sure they are fleshed out and depicted as the multi-dimensional beings that they truly are.

Point of View

Distinctive characters are clear and distinctive because they have clear points of view. Clear points of view derive from how characters see the world, what they want, and what they struggle with. Don't confuse characteristics with point of view. Telling us a character is a teenager, stoner, old, Black, Jewish, female, poor, a politician, gay, or struggling with their weight does not tell us who they are or how they feel and think.

Are They Emotionally Engaging?

While the characters may not be the main focus of a movie, they should still be engaging and distinctive. Even in a 95-person opus like the final *Avengers* movie, we still know the origin story of each superhero, who they love, what their weaknesses are, that some are pure and idealistic, others are snarky, and some go rogue.

We emotionally engage with characters when we can identify with their goal and their wants. It may not be what we all want, but at least we should understand their deeper desire. They want to win a drumming competition and while we might not drum, we understand wanting to excel at something. We'll engage more if they are three-dimensional and have flaws that we can we identify with. (They want to be a songwriter but self-sabotage). We'll emotionally invest if they battle obstacles, since we also have obstacles. In real life, I may give up in the face of an obstacle whether it's related to my career, love life, type of lifestyle, or anything else. But we all want to emotionally invest in stories about people that don't give up. Especially once we understand their reasons and stakes.

Dream Small?

Look at Leslie Knope from *Parks and Recreation*. The writers gave her the smallest, most unidentifiable TV series goal in season one. A woman — who isn't even the head of Parks and Recreation but an assistant, and not in a big city, but a small town in Indiana — wants to fill a hole (literally, not emotionally) in a yard. And maybe make a park. That's it. However, the character wants it so badly and has such a passionate and refreshing POV, that we root for her.

If I pitched "The small town assistant head of Parks and Recreation wants to fill a dirt hole in a very small town…" it may not start a bidding war but once we see that character's unstoppable optimism, her commitment to a better world, her awkwardness, and her big dreams — we get it. We've seen "good politicians" before, but Leslie Knope is distinctive, and based on her passion for parks and people, we emotionally invest.

Do They Have External and Internal Arcs?

Whether we're writing or criticizing a character, it's critical to ensure that they have external *and* internal arcs. We should track them pursuing something big (whether it's clearly big, like acquiring a billion-dollar painting, or a character's particular passion, like Leslie Knope filling dirt in a hole) and as they do, we should also track a personal change or transformation that results from said pursuit.

External Goals

It's easy to track an external goal or arc. The character wants to win the love interest, and by the end of the story we'll know if they've achieved that or not. Also, the external goal can change. The goal can start out being what they *think* they want, (to win the lottery) but then, interweaving with the internal arc, change into getting what they *need* (to accept themselves, flaws and all.)

The best external goals have clear *personal* stakes for the main characters. If they want to rob multiple casinos we'll root for them to get it (like in *Ocean's Eleven*, because we get into the cleverness of the plot and details and hey, it's a heist movie). But if they want to rob casinos so they can afford heart surgery for their mother, we'll root even harder.

Internal Changes

We also want to track their internal arcs. What do they learn, heal, confront, face, accept, or relinquish about themselves, their point of view, or life itself over the course of the story? That arc starts with a flaw — one that they don't deal with or acknowledge, or that holds them back or gets them the wrong things. We should learn about this flaw very early in the film. By the end of Act One/first 30 minutes in a movie, they're not facing this flaw yet. By the midpoint/about 60 minutes in, there's a crack. They see another way to be and either take that in or reject it, but they haven't changed yet. By the end of Act Two/around 90 minutes in, that stubbornness, blind spot, or weakness has contributed to the "all is low point."

Three-Act Structure

Most feature films have a three-act structure. Act One sets up the world, characters, conflict, and quest. Act Two is where conflicts, plots, and subplots escalate. By the end of Act Two, all seems lost. Act Three is where the protagonist finally heals, transforms, and faces their inner demons. They then fight their biggest battle and achieve some sort of resolution. For now, know that while those are the guidelines for the external plot, they also help us track a character's internal arc or journey as well.

More About Act Three Internal Resolutions

In Act Three, main characters must face what they never faced about themselves or have transformed within themselves enough to finally fight their biggest internal and external battles. For example, in a romance they might need to become a better person, apologize to those they've wronged, or deal with an issue within themselves that they've never been complete with. Or even be willing to sacrifice the love interest for a greater good...

They may not get what they want, but perhaps they'll get what they need. And sometimes they don't get that either, which defines a tragedy over a comedy. Charles Foster Kane died alone.

Rainman's Brother?

A great example of an easy character arc to track is in the movie *Rainman*. I don't mean Dustin Hoffman's character, but Charles Babbit, the character played by Tom Cruise. In the opening, he's greedy, selfish, and we can tell what he needs by how he treats his girlfriend. He *needs* to open up and care about people, but he *wants* money. This impatient, non-people person is then given the worst (and best) thing for him: he's put in a car on a road trip with an autistic brother who keeps a rigid schedule. This is the last thing Charlie would want and the only thing that can give him what he needs. We then track their relationship arc as well as Charlie's internal arc and can measure how he's changed in the end by two things: one, he now treats his girlfriend better. And two, he cares about his brother more than money.

We track his *internal arc* by *external measures*. The road trip with the brother to find money was the external journey. His discovering, using, bonding, learning from, and then loving his brother (and his girlfriend) is his internal journey.

Arcs for Secondary Characters

Often, smaller characters can act as benchmarks or be a little less developed than the main characters. But if they have sizeable roles then it would be best for them to have their own stories and arcs. If good-time stoner guy goes off on a road trip with the three main characters, maybe he just offers comic relief. But if it's just one main character and the stoner is the second lead, they should have an internal journey of his own. Remember, it adds nuances and levels to the script, and it helps attract talent to have strong secondary characters with their own stories.

If they are tiny characters, like the old lady who states it's going rain because her corns are throbbing, she may just be a set up for a pay off. (More on those later). And "Stoner #8" might not need a lot of development but supporting characters do. If the main character in high school wants to date a hot guy, then the secondary character should help or hinder them *while also pursuing a goal of their own*. Then the arcs of both characters can inform each other, thematically relate, help build subplots, and result in a more complex story.

When the Sidekick Is Just a Device

We often meet secondary characters in a script who feel like "cheerleaders" or "sidekicks" for the main character. They don't have their own stories, and they often come across more as a device, than a full-fledged character.

I call them the "How's it going?" character. Say we have a story where the protagonist likes the popular boy, and so we have a couple of scenes where a friend hangs out, calls, or appears solely to have a "How's it going with Dwight?" conversation. This allows the main character to vent or express themselves. Then the friend character goes into a box and are pulled out later to ask once again, "How's it going with Dwight?" These characters are one-dimensional, have no life of their own, but might have a funny line or tick.

And these flat characters don't always have to be positive and helpful — they can also be the "jeerleaders." You know, like Nelson, the "Haha!" character that works as a running gag on the *Simpsons*. But if they have a larger role to play, they should have their own subplot and story. They could be the rival for the love interest or job, they could be a coworker or someone who isn't rooting for the main character. But just like the above "How's it going" character examples, "Jeerleaders" can't just appear, do their thing, and go into a box until they're needed again. Track them. Give them their own stories and layers.

Longer Arcs in TV Shows

Since a TV series may span numerous seasons, a character's arc may take longer. One hour-dramas like *The Sopranos*, *Euphoria*, or *Breaking Bad* can spend seasons on the transformations (both good and bad) in their main characters.

However, in many broadcast half-hour sitcoms, main characters often resist change and remain loveable but stubborn (Peter from *Family Guy* won't really change). Or they can change but only over a long time. Archie Bunker, TV's most famous bigot, got his values handed back to him time and time again, and stayed who he was for the most part. On the rare occasions when he did care or take a different POV, it was momentous.

Are They Three-Dimensional?

We want characters to be complex, but don't assume a writer is green (new) or lazy if their characters are clichéd, a bit superficial, or one-dimensional. The writer might not be aware that their characters come off as simplistic. Perhaps, as stated above, they're writing about someone they know, but they can't get out of their fixed view of that person. Maybe their character is based on a narcissistic friend, and that's all the writer can see. Or maybe they assume that the genre doesn't call for much development. "He's an axe murderer. Put an axe in his hand, make him mean, and have him do some murders. Done."

Sometimes we've seen a certain character so often, it's like shorthand:

> A middle school nerd that no one pays attention to.
> The corrupt politician, CEO, etc.

A sexy-as-hell vampire.

These can come off as clichés, and "too familiar and not different." Make them complex by giving them a distinctive point of view. For example, "a recently widowed and corrupt politician who now must be the sole parent to his 6-year-old son."

What is the unique point of view of this character? What are their gifts and flaws? Their internal and external conflicts? What makes them tick? What are their hot button issues? What is their background? Most importantly, what can audiences identify with?

Surpassing Expectations in *Juno*

Juno is about a sarcastic teen who gets pregnant. But she's subtly nuanced. She wants the perfect family for her baby — wants it to have love — and yet can't bring herself to admit she loves Bleeker. She's tough on the outside while both metaphorically and literally, her insides are completely out of her control.

In *Juno,* the secondary characters are nuanced as well. There's the dad that supports her and doesn't want to kill Bleeker; the supportive stepmother; and Bleeker, the father of the baby, who is the nicest kid on the planet.

In *How to Get Away with Murder* the characters are flawed and navigate their moral codes as they study law. Viola Davis' character tries to do what's best and pretends she knows what's best but she has drinking issues, intimacy issues, and power issues. She's flawed. We love her powerful moments, huge breakdowns, and how she constantly worries about making everyone's life worse.

These characters are nuanced, complex, have strong points of view, and numerous strengths and flaws. They're human. And that helps audiences identify with them.

Anti-Heroes and Villains We Love to Hate

Many people credit *The Sopranos* with the rise of the anti-hero, but of course there have been many beforehand. Look at *Frankenstein.* We care for the monster because he's an outcast, lonely, and tragic. Tony Soprano was another kind of monster, but he loved his family and of course, some ducks. (And it was interesting to hear his POV in therapy.) Walter White from *Breaking Bad* turned a lot of people off as time went on, but we saw where he came from, how weak he once was, and how he wanted to provide for his family. As he became corrupt, audiences' sympathy may have changed into shock and fascination, yet he remained compelling.

There's a fine line between loving/hating a character and losing sympathy with them. There's no exact science, but we know it when we see it. A character does something and loses the audience. It could be that they kill an animal or commit some crime, aggression, or have an attitude that people can't get over. Sometimes a good writer can make us see life through such a character's eyes for a moment and that scares the hell out of us. The series *Dexter* did this well, using voice-over that contrasted with his heinous activities. There's nothing like watching a serial killer saw through body parts while reminding himself to pick up dinner for his girlfriend and her kids. He also had a code of conduct and struggled with a vicious addiction. The former made us sort of forgive him, while the latter gave us a thread of understanding.

So, we can love a villain. We can relate to their flaws and so can our inner monsters. We can also root for them to change or simply admire how they "break bad" for as long as they can.

Is the Protagonist Active?

This may seem obvious but sometimes it's not as clear as one would think. Often, a protagonist is acted upon rather than active. In other words, other characters have goals and the protagonist goes along with them.

A note I often give is to not have "lucky" protagonists — where people and things suddenly appear and help these characters out in the nick of time. We want protagonists to *cause* their own victories and losses as much as possible.

This does not mean that they do things alone. And as I'll get into later, *set ups* and *pay offs* can help things seem less contrived, lucky or coincidental. But as far as main events go, we need our characters to drive those events, provide momentum, and be active (rather than passive) characters.

Also, never focus on what a character doesn't want, focus on what they do want. Have them pursue something and take actions towards it, even if it's the wrong thing. They should make a decision and put something into action.

Always assess if characters are causing their own wins, losses, and resolution — whether tragic or not.

One issue that often occurs is when the arc of a main character takes them from being controlled to taking control, or if they are indecisive and become decisive. While that is a valid arc, it can be hard to write successfully. In order to work, those types of characters must somehow be reactive people who are also active characters.

But *The Graduate...*?

Consider *The Graduate*, where even the logline is passive:

> A disillusioned college graduate finds himself torn between his older lover and her daughter.

In this case Benjamin Braddock is stuck in his life, is acted upon by Mrs. Robinson, and somehow ends up pursuing her daughter. It's a bit rough as far as active protagonists go, but Ben *pursues a distraction* (an affair with Mrs. Robinson) to escape his indecision about the future (becoming an adult). This is an example of a passive person that still actively drives the plot.

Will Actors Want to Play Them?

Here's a question I rarely considered in the beginning of my writing career but it's something both writers and Readers should consider. When crafting coverage for a writer, Readers should look and see if these are roles that well-established actors might want to play. Since we're often reading for buyers or sellers, when covering a script for development, the potential for great casting is considered crucial.

A-list talent = $$, and well-written, nuanced characters help attract them.

What types of characters do actors want to play? Three-dimensional, complex, messy, active characters, with strong arcs. And by messy, I mean complex. Not *one* thing, multiples! Rage, guilt, shame, *and* frustration. A term tossed around in Hollywood is "Oscar bait," which means the kind of role that could get someone nominated for an award. Unique characters, complicated backstories, people who have contradictions, layers and depth, maybe even grey moral areas, etc. Us humans on an average day.

There are also times when people want to play a character regardless of how unnuanced they are. For example, Robert Redford wanted to play a "baddie" in an *Avengers* movie for his grandchildren. Or someone wants to drive a fast and furious car for a big paycheck. Or both — Brie Larson played *Captain Marvel* (not just for a big paycheck, she's a freaking bad-ass female superhero) and then the lead in *Room* (a bad-ass mom and a complex, nuanced, and messy character — winning the Oscar for Best Actress).

To recap: Whether writing a script, or writing coverage, look to see if the characters are complex and intriguing enough to attract talent. Actors don't want to play one-note, passive people. Which brings us to...

Flaws and Strengths

Good characters need clear flaws and strengths. An action hero is more interesting if they are flawed, and a villain shouldn't just be "bad." Strengths make characters likeable and give them tools to navigate their upcoming journey. Flaws make characters relatable, give them nuances, a place to go, and a way to grow. They allow us to see ourselves and sympathize with characters. Flaws and strengths should be crafted subtly, tracked, and utilized.

Appropriate to the Time and Place

Characters should fit the time and place, which can be defined by the following:

Codes of Conduct

Would the characters have rules and codes in the world they live in, and do they act accordingly?

Superheroes and vampires have codes. So does Dexter. So does a marine sergeant. So do characters in *Straight Outta Compton* and the kids in *Stranger Things*. Writers can't assume that audiences will know what the codes and rules are, so hopefully they take time to establish them. For example, in some movies, superheroes save the world, while in others they must hide because super beings have been outlawed.

Setting Specifics

What about setting? Do the characters act and talk like people of that planet, region, group, or time? And while most writers know not to have a cowboy in an 1880's western twerk, sometimes this issue is more subtle than that.

People of other times, regions, groups, and worlds might have codes, but more often they have a mindset and we need to know what that mindset is. I recently heard someone say not to assume that people in the past were less intelligent than we are. This is just one example of creating a realistic mindset for a character from another time or place.

Mind the Mindsets

When I speak of a character's mindset, it's a combination of many elements. Writers have to get into those mindsets, whether their characters come from a different time, place or point of view.

Sometimes the errors are subtle. For example, the sensitive, feminist, male writer of today crafting a sympathetic, feminist, male supporter of the Suffragettes in the 1920's would have a different vocabulary, understanding, and set of considerations.

Most writers craft characters who are different than themselves so they must remember that their characters don't just have different voices and dialogue, they also have different values, strengths, weaknesses, arcs, codes, opportunities, and perspectives.

Would They Really Do That?

Characters should grow, evolve, and change, but that's different from being inconsistent with what's been established. Once we've established a character, are their actions in line with the character we created? Are the characters consistent?

Good example: It's great that the grumpy soccer player Roy Kent in *Ted-Lasso* has a little niece that he sits and reads to. That makes him complex and layered.

Not so good example: A bold and courageous suffragette suddenly announces that women should be seen and not heard.

Often when reading scripts, I find myself thinking a character has switched up too drastically or I've come to know them in one way and now their words, actions, or behavior have done a complete 180. And let me reiterate — I don't mean growth or adding layers. A frightened character should gain courage — gradually. But if a character is timid in the opening, and by page ten gives a huge speech to the entire nation, we better see them struggle with that speech. They can't just do it confidently and then suddenly be timid again.

Too Many People, One Voice

I once worked with a writer who knew the world of addicts in a small town. He wrote the struggles and perspectives in ways I could not. The characters were wonderfully flawed, raw, harsh, and realistic. And then there were the women. Just like his main character, this writer might have been too self-absorbed or too focused on addiction to really understand anything else. Three-dimensional female characters were beyond him.

Many people tried to help. Everyone had an opinion of what to do and the writer followed their advice, tweaking things in one direction and then another. We went through various iterations and it never seemed to improve, and the project eventually felt apart.

We all can easily write some types of characters but not others. We can do research, but it might not be enough. If a character is different than us, we must figure out how to get into their world and portray their POV. Writers must go into their core to write the character they always wanted to be or dread they are — and show us all we're not alone in our hopes and dreams. Actors want to play that.

Readers, did they accomplish that and if not, how can we help?

Exercises

1. Craft a character based on a person you know.

   Think of a real person in your life. Describe them on the page. Try to convey the following:

   A. Physical attributes (what do they look like)

   B. Mental attributes (How smart are they? What do they think about?)

   C. Emotional components: (Are they confident, insecure, depressed, happy, jealous, etc.)

   D. Goals and fears: What do they want and how badly do they want it? What do they fear, how strongly do they fear it and why?

   E. Strengths and weaknesses. What are they good at and what are they not so good at? Where do they have room to grow?

   F. Background: (Rich, poor, age, where are they from? Childhood?)

   You can do this as a list, a paragraph or a chart.

2. Craft a character that is fictitious.

   Now do the same thing for a made-up character. You make them up. Don't take them from fiction. But answer the same A-F questions above.

   Which was easier to write? Basing a character on a real person or making one up? Everyone's answers are different and that's how we get Jerry Seinfeld writing about himself and his friends vs. something like *The Avengers*.

3. Imagine your two characters in a scene together.

   What situation could these two characters find themselves in? For example, if I wrote about my mother in exercise one, and a Roman soldier in exercise two, either my mother or the soldier might travel through time and meet each other, or I can imagine my mother in that time period, possibly as the mother of the soldier before he goes off to war.

   Come up with at least five scenarios that the two characters might find themselves in. What would their different POV's be? What conflicts might arise? What could they learn or help each other with?

7

Story

Theirs vs. Yours

The story-related items that buyers and sellers look for or want their Readers to analyze include such questions as, is the plot clear? Logical? Focused? Also, if the logline intrigued them, does the story live up to their expectations?

In addition to these big story questions, Readers will often make story-related notes that arise from the specific project they're reading. For example, a Reader may write something like, "If she just lost her husband of fifteen years, why doesn't anyone address that in the following scenes?" In other words, there's no rule that says, "If someone breaks up with their husband of fifteen years, they must address it in the following scenes."

This chapter will include tips and guidelines, but there are fewer rules of the trade, since most comments and questions about a script's story will differ based on the issues that pop up on a case-by-case basis.

I'd also like to address the subheading of the chapter — their story vs. your story. As Readers, we must make sure that our notes on a writer's story are just that — notes on their story — not the story we would have written. This sounds basic, but subjectivity is a sneaky little bug. We must assume that what we're reading is the story the writer wants to tell and figure out how to help them get their vision out as clearly as possible.

So going forward in this chapter, remember the following items:

> **Story notes are usually based on how a particular story** is being told and are crafted on a case-by-case basis.
>
> **Readers help make the writer's story as clear** and strong as possible.

Logic

When reading a script, logic issues are easy to find. They're those problems that leave us confused and make us go back and check something that was established earlier. When this occurs, a Reader (and eventually someone watching the movie) can get pulled out of the story.

As Readers giving notes on logic, try to point out what isn't clear followed by comments about what might help.

Fictional Worlds and Their Rules

Every story has rules that govern its world. As Readers, we need to ensure that, based on the rules of the world that the writer has set up, do the characters, plot, and story make sense?

The easiest type of script to read is one set in the present day and in a realistic world that we all know and live in. If we open a script and the slugline reads:

```
EXT. NEW YORK CITY - DAY
```

...then we're probably fine. This will likely be a familiar world or some form of it. Genres like science fiction, fantasy, fairy tale, supernatural, and horror must invent worlds and the rules that govern them, alongside characters, and situations.

Think of a show like *True Blood*. It's set in the deep South and includes vampires, werewolves, and other supernatural creatures. But the pilot starts with a news report that lets us know that vampires live amongst humans in this world and that there's something manufactured that they can drink instead of actual blood. Without this setup, Readers (and audiences) would get confused and then likely lose interest because the scenes that follow would not make sense. Note that just because vampires are a well-known type of mythical being, that doesn't mean the rules about how specific vampires live can be inferred. *Twilight* and *Vampire Diaries* came out around the same time as *True Blood*, but they did not all follow the same set of vampire rules. As a Reader, make sure that each script that involves building a world defines its own rules.

Here is an example of a note I wrote on for a screenplay with world-building issues:

> When writing fantastical, science fiction or surreal stories, the audience will need a little extra help understanding the circumstances, world and all its rules. We open with the protagonist as a child, and that's a good prologue, but then we go to some surreal type of incident and then a realistic one. We see the child levitate and then sitting in rehab. We need more information and a clearer context early on.

Another instance where we'll need help understanding the world is when a script is set in a historical time period. Knowing that *Masters of Sex* takes place in the 1950's helps explain why a married man who wants to curb his homosexual feelings would volunteer for electroshock therapy. Readers should note whether or not the writer knows the time period and its ways, and has set them up clearly and distinctly.

Plot Holes

A plot hole is simply a flaw in the logic of the world of the script. If the head of the Mafia tells his son, Phil, that he's going to be the new Don, but then later we see the middle son, Phineas, running things, we recognize a logical inconsistency. Why is Phineas in control? We have a hole in the plot.

Plot holes are one of the items that are adjudicated on a case-by-case basis. Once in a while we'll flip back to earlier sections in the script to see if we missed something, and if we didn't then we can comment on it:

> On page 16 Don Antonio promised his son, Phil, that he could be the new Don, but then on page 67, he gives the title to Phil's younger brother, Phineas. If something changed, it should be mentioned. If not, then clarify why this occurred.

There are many "why" or "how" questions that come up in story notes. Readers will find themselves asking a writer to justify choices or clarify a situation. Also, sometimes the story jumps from one situation to another and could use a beat or transition in between.

Consistency

Often there are story consistency questions that might also fall into the character or dialogue category in a coverage template. For example, if a character said he was unemployed, then why do we see him at work? This could be a story, dialogue, or character issue. It's our choice as a Reader to decide how to label it.

Here's an example of a quick logic note/question I gave to a writer once:

> The Girl was moving to England forever and only had one suitcase?

In some scripts, that situation might be just fine. In the context of this one, it was confusing and noticing it stopped the flow of the plot.

Does All This Apply to Comedies?

One logic note I find myself giving quite often is regarding broad comedies (*The Hangover, Wedding Crashers, Airplane,* etc.) which are often sillier and less grounded in reality. While there can be some bending in the logic rules, those rules shouldn't be broken. Broad comedies might jump from one situation to another or have funny repartee, but things still must make sense within its world. Although audiences will laugh at a silly situation, they still need to believe what's going on and invest in the reality of the story.

We'll only suspend disbelief if there is some acknowledgement of the unbelievable thing. For example, if we're talking about a big fart joke movie, and the writer sets up beforehand that a character has the ability to fart for ten minutes uninterrupted, then I'll go along with it.

I always say, address (or have one character address) a question an audience may have, and then move on:

> CHRIS
> Why can you fart for ten minutes long, Joe?
>
> JOE
> I am made of beans and prunes.

Originality

As a Reader, when assessing the story of a script, we'll need to give some thought to the script's originality. Are there elements we've seen before? Can they be heightened or given a unique spin?

This means that Readers need to do some homework and keep up with current films and TV series. Reading "the trades" (*Variety, Deadline, The Hollywood Reporter*) is the best way to stay aware of what's already been made.

Lack of originality isn't always bad. In Chapter 4, "Loglines" I explained that the film industry loves situations that are familiar yet different. Nowhere is that more obvious than in all the "reboots" of old films and TV series.

But even reboots need to feel original in some way. The first couple of *Spider-Man* movies were kind of distinct from each other. Many that followed used the same formula, but with younger actors. And then came *Spider-Man: Into the Spider-Verse*. This was a very different story and take involving an ethnically diverse kid rather than the usual white, teenage boy. In addition, it was animated and the story explored other dimensions.

Engaging the Audience

Executives hear pitches all day. They want to become engrossed and they will be when the story has passion, a universal theme, and someone or something that grips them, wakes them up, makes them laugh, cry, wonder or think.

A story is usually engaging if:

- It has sympathetic characters.
- It has high stakes.
- We can understand and identify with the personal motivations of the characters.
- The characters show us a new angle, aspect or POV we haven't seen before.
- The world of the story is riveting.
- The relationships are intricate.
- There are internal and external character arcs.
- The obstacles are huge.

Sometimes a writer plays it too safe. They don't get their protagonist into enough trouble, they don't throw enough rocks at them, or the characters are "lucky" and have things work out for them. While *My Big Fat Greek Wedding* was quite enjoyable and successful, one missing story element is that the couple's marriage never seemed to be in jeopardy. The story mainly focused on how annoying or irritating the woman's family was.

There are many things to consider when assessing whether a script has that "It" factor, but the main thing is to ask is, "Do I care? Did I get lost? Hooked? Taken on a journey?" When a movie begins we all recognize that what we're about to see is fake, but once our emotions are engaged, we forget that and go along for the ride.

Readers (and writers) must determine whether the script they're reading (or writing) does that. Why or why not? Start noticing.

Not Enough Details

One common story-related note is that something is too subtle and needs clarifying. Or sometimes it's the opposite problem: something is too detailed and needs less clarifying. Writers have blind spots. They know the story, but we don't. They may think they're being clear when we actually need more information. And sometimes they bombard us with too much information and need to learn to trust the audience and scale back.

All writers start with a vision. They put it in a screenplay and hope the audience understands that vision. But darn those pesky audience members! They have their own interpretations, points of view, and visions. Therefore, as Readers, we must help the writer get their vision across as clearly as possible.

While covering a script recently, I came across a character who went to a seedy company to ask questions about it. They were then offered a job there. I commented that we might need a bit more information on how the writer jumped from a character inquiring about the company to being asked to work there. Were the people desperate to hire someone? Did they see something in that character? And why did the character accept? We didn't get enough information on her financial situation, personality, or backstory to know why she'd work there.

Too Many Details

As a Reader for the entertainment industry, most of the scripts we read are intended for a large, mainstream audience. Consequently, we can ask ourselves, "Will normal people understand, grasp, and follow what's going on in the script?"

Some scripts might have military personnel, doctors, scientists, or other experts who use technical jargon in a way that leaves the audience confused. Readers should note when explanations for technical jargon are needed. Similarly, the audience might need to know all of the steps in an elaborate plan. If two characters mention how their town has gone to the dogs, we want to know what happened. We'll need more information, but we also don't want a four-page lecture on the real estate by-laws that ruined the town.

Specific story details in scripts can help paint pictures in our mind, as well as help us emotionally invest and draw us in. But too many can alienate us.

I once had a Reader comment that there was too much sex in a script. I asked them if that was a personal reaction, or whether there might be a demographic and audience for the script they were covering that didn't include them. Did the sex seem gratuitous and only there for shock value? Did it impede the plot, or were they just uncomfortable? In this case, the Reader said that the sex overwhelmed the plot and didn't inform character. I advised that they could state that as a possible consideration. Otherwise, the Reader needed to judge the story for what it was: an explicit teenage love story.

But Beverly, What Do You Look For?

Thanks for asking. Here are some questions I ask and items I look for when assessing a script's story and plot. These things are hallmarks of a good story.

- Is the story believable? (Again, according to the rules established within the story itself.)
- Does the story establish a certain tone, genre, or reality and then suddenly switch?
- Are there layers, complexities, twists, and turns? Are they predictable? Set up properly?
- Are the stakes high? Can they be elevated?
- Is the goal clear? Does it change? Meaning does the goal evolve (which is good) vs. just sort of change and the protagonist forgets it and goes for something very different (not as good)?
- Are the obstacles big and do they escalate?
- Is there enough conflict?
- Is there enough tension?
- Are subplots relevant and do they develop and resolve?
- Does the writer "show" vs. "tell"?
- Are conflicts resolved or are there loose ends? It's fine to leave a cliffhanger for a sequel, but are the main set-ups paid off/resolved by the end and are most questions addressed?
- Is there a strong enough story engine? Do we find ourselves invested in an engaging protagonist-driven plot?
- Do we understand the choices characters make? Do we need more information or a clearer context?

You Had Me at Hello! and Lost Me at *"It Was All a Dream"*

As Readers, there will be scripts that make us angry. This usually happens when we get invested and then things seem to drop off, don't follow the rules, or don't get addressed. I'm not exaggerating, it can make us angry because the writer did a good job but didn't follow through. We must take our anger out somewhere in a nice healthy manner and give an objective, professional note. And again, we can't state where *we* want to see the story go, we must objectively have a sense of where the story seemed to be going and then took an abrupt turn. There is a difference between surprises and twists, and things that are inconsistent or just not dealt with.

The classic example of this is when the script takes us along an amazing adventure and then the character wakes up and we learn it was all a dream.

I've been invested in a story where it seemed that the main character would die if they didn't get their goal, then they didn't get it and it wasn't a big deal. I felt cheated somehow.

What if we did think the head of the mafia was going to name his son, Phil, the new Don? And we really invested in Phil, and yet he just up and gave it to his younger son, Phineas and the reasons why were never addressed? We might feel confused, betrayed and frustrated.

Stay objective and give the note about wanting to see something resolved. It doesn't have to be a happy ending with a bow on it — just addressed and acknowledged.

After all, we want our movies to wrap things up, since life doesn't always do that.

Exercises

1. Justifying logic: Below I have written two scenarios that take a wrong turn. Come up with three ways to justify how or why this wrong turn happened.

   For example: If the head of the mafia promised to make his son, Phil, the new leader, and halfway through, he anoints the younger brother, Phineas, as the new Don instead…

   Perhaps:

   A. Phil is killed before that can happen and now the title must go to the next in line, Phineas.

   B. Like the old biblical story, Isaac, Jacob and Esau, perhaps the Don is blind and accidentally appoints the wrong son.

C.   Maybe Phineas is weaker, and a rival gang forces the Don to give the title to him rather than Phil, so their own gang can be stronger.

Give it a try:

> **First Scenario**: At the opening of a film, two very poor teenage girls work at a 7-11. Later, we see that one is in a rocket ship, going off to space. Justify how this might occur.
>
> **Second Scenario**: A woman cradles her newborn child with her adoring husband. 30 pages later she's in an underground prison cell in Croatia. Justify how she might have ended up there.

2. Raising stakes: If a character doesn't care about their goal, neither will the audience. In order for a plot to engage us, the goal must have high stakes — obtaining the goal is a huge accomplishment, and/or not obtaining it will have dire consequences. (For example: if a superhero doesn't defeat a supervillain, the planet may be destroyed.)

Let's say that a teenage protagonist wants to get a job at Burger King. The stakes aren't given and so the goal doesn't seem that big. But if I add that the teenage protagonist wants to get out of their small town and needs to go on the senior trip to NY where they will stay, not return, and try to become a Broadway actor — then working at Burger King is a big deal because it's a step towards a new future. And it doesn't even have to be a step. I could say — he wants to get a job at Burger King to finally separate from his family, who for generations, worked at McDonalds. (And thus begins the great 21st century Burger Wars).

Here are two scenarios of goals with low stakes. Add some detail or details to raise the stakes and make these more interesting.

> **First scenario:** A woman working in the payroll department of an office wants to transfer to human resources. Come up with three different ways to raise the stakes:
>
> **Second scenario:** A child wants to play outside. Come up with three different ways to raise the stakes:

3. Change a goal from *doesn't want* to *want*: Protagonists must actively pursue a goal. Too often we see that they don't want something, which makes them avoid situations and wait to *be acted upon* by others, etc. They don't *cause* events, they *respond* to events. We have to turn the "no" into a "yes" and change what they don't want into what they do want. For example:

Instead of:

> A gang member doesn't want to be in a gang anymore.

This doesn't tell us what they're going for — only what they may be running from, which makes them passive characters. Think of what they want to do instead and have them go for that. One example could be:

> A gang member wants to leave a gang and go to California to be with a girl he's never stopped loving.

Now we see what he might do and why.

Here are three passive, or "don't want," scenarios. Come up with a way to make each of these active and write what the protagonist *does want*.

> **First scenario**: The valedictorian of a high school is sick of (doesn't want/like) living a sheltered life.
>
> **Second scenario**: Everyone pressures a reluctant (they don't want it) politician to run for president.
>
> **Third scenario**: A day care center is closing and the local parents are bummed (don't want that to happen).

4. Logic and world-building: Watch the first ten minutes (up to the inciting incidents) of three different films or TV shows that occurred in a time before now. For each, notice if and how the writer lets you know the setting, time, and location, of the story. Pay attention to how this is revealed. Is this information conveyed directly, like inserting the time and location in words on the screen? Or maybe a character is shown looking at a newspaper headline with a date, or the date is mentioned in dialogue? Or is this information revealed indirectly, maybe by showing old cars, a pirate ship, or some other element of a previous time? Notice if you're satisfied, or if you want to know more. As I stated, seeing a pirate ship with old time pirates may be enough (17th-19th centuries?) Seeing a black woman turned away at the polling place, might lead to assume the story is set before 1969, but do you need more information?

5. Too many/not enough details: What more would you need to know if you read the following first pages of some different scripts.

```
INT. JAIL CELLS — DAY

A THROBBING DARK ORB with a police cap
and smoking a cigar, leans menacingly
against the bars of a cell, taunting a
BIG GORILLA with a red cape and boots and
giant CO on its chest.

                    ORB
          Finally. The world will see the
          pathetic Captain Orangutang
          executed before its very eyes. And
          you are just the first!
```

EXT. TURQUOISE PLANET — NIGHT

A gaseous, extremely large planet rotates
on its axis very quickly.

EXT. PLANET'S STREETS — NIGHT

HADI OBADOR, (30's), runs for his life.
The Kraptex squad was after him. He
clutches an orb and throws it into the
sky where it's sucked up by a gaseous
windstorm.

EXT. ANCIENT HARAPPA — DAY

A SMALL MAN, (30's), brings steatite
seals to his sun-dried brick home and
enters.

INT. BRICK HOME — CONTINUOUS

                SMALL MAN
          Wife? Wife?

No one is there. Pots are broken on the
dirt floor. Barley thrown and thrashed
around.

                SMALL MAN (CONT'D)
          NO! NO! War has come!

8

Structure

A Formula? But I'm an Arteest!

There is a bit of a formula to a screenplay structure.

I have seen the horrified look in some people's eyes when they are told that there is a well-known and widely adopted formula to structuring screenplays and teleplays. I understand. People want to see themselves as artists. They want to go with the flow, follow the muse, write a screenplay like a Jackson Pollack painting.

I will now quote my mother, Phyllis Neufeld's Golden Rule that I got at age 16: There's a way to drive for the driving test and there's a way to drive for life. Ergo, learn the rules and then (and only then) can we break them.

Throw Out the Books, Classes, and Lectures, and Never Cite Them

Every book on screenwriting will give out some hard and fast rules. Some books will preach them like the gospel. However, after learning these rules, Readers shouldn't preach them back in the coverage.

For example, don't say:

> As Syd Field always says, you need to have an inciting incident...

You'll sound like you're in a cult, or you can't think for yourself. At worst it will come across like lecturing.

Instead, just address the issue:

> By page ten there should be an inciting incident to indicate where the main plot may be headed.

Readers don't have to state where they learned this — they are the authority.

What is a Mark?

I'll go into each of these *marks* in detail in the next section, but here's a quick cheat sheet for the structure of most feature films. The page numbers are guidelines and may change for shorter or longer scripts:

- Page 1 is the opening. Create a strong first impression.

- Page 10 is the inciting incident. Something needs to shift by this point.

- Page 25-30 is the end of Act One. The protagonist should be pursuing a goal

- Page 60 is the midpoint. Stakes and obstacles are escalating, and the main character may get a glimpse of a new way of being or thinking but doesn't quite change yet.

- Page 90 is the end of Act Two. All should seem lost,

- Somewhere between 90-120 pages is Act Three: the biggest battles, the protagonist may finally transform, and cause their resolution in the end.

Hitting the Marks and Why?

The rules for screenwriting that are hammered into every new writer's head have become the standard for a reason. Some executives and Readers really will decide whether or not they like a script by the first, fifth, or tenth page. If a script is not doing what it should on those pages, then an executive may not even finish reading it.

As I showed in the sample templates in Chapter 2, many companies ask for comments on structure. And while there are basic questions that always arise, such as, "Do conflicts escalate?" "Does it move well?" and "Do the characters change?", many also want to know if it hits *the marks*. Why? Because, for the most part, the marks work.

If, when reading a script, we can feel in our gut that something is off or isn't engaging, then the script probably isn't hitting one of the marks or it's not hitting it at the appropriate moment.

Formulas, guidelines, and standards are there to ensure that scripts feel like the audience is taken on a spontaneous roller coaster ride., In reality, of course, there's nothing spontaneous about it — the script has been carefully crafted to make the audience feel that way.

The formulas and marks will:

Get the audience on a ride right away, ramp the ride up, keep it going, escalate, weave, twist, turn, surprise, shock, then send them physically and emotionally crashing to rock bottom. They'll worry they'll never get out, then they'll churn, churn, churn, change, slowly climb back up, and plunge into the biggest, most thrilling part of the ride, before being deposited back, seemingly where they started, but actually in a different place — where they are changed forever and in a new and better way.

These rules exist regardless of genre. There's one type of roller coaster for a romantic-comedy and another for an adventure/quest, but no matter what the story is about, with proper structuring, the ride can be exhilarating.

So now, let's look more closely at what those marks are.

How to Get the Reader or Executive to Keep Going After Page 1, 5, or 10

I can't express enough how many executives and agents feel like Sisyphus, pushing a rock up a hill, or Lucy and Ethel with the never-ending conveyor belt of chocolates coming at them, simply because of the huge volume of scripts they receive. Writing competitions are the same. Let's say 6000 people (of all levels) enter.

In both situations, our job as Readers is to advance the best.

Most Readers are required to read a script from beginning to end. Occasionally, an agent/exec puts it down because it doesn't hook them early, however, *most* execs and *all* Readers continue reading, because coverage must be written and logged into a database. Even if we've decided the script is not great early on, we will still read it so we can write a complete coverage. So Readers must see a script through till the end — but first impressions can be hard to undo.

Before the Beginning

How early can that first impression be made? Sooner than one would think. From a stack of screenplays, a prejudice can come from a title, the length, if there are typos, and so on. All those judgments occur before the Reader gets into the content.

Look at this batch of screenplay titles and subjectively, what are our first impressions? (I'm just making some up here):

> *Milo Gets a Haircut*
> *Love & Warthog Maintenance*
> *406,201 Molecular Inconsistencies*
> *Space Vampires in the Year 1865*
> *The Untold Story of Adolph Hitler's Real Plans*

We can't help it. We already have an opinion… *because we're human.*

Knowing that a feature screenplay should be about 90-120 pages or so (remember, that's a guideline, not a commandment), what would a Reader think when handed a 210-page script (not written by Martin Scorsese) or even a 64-page one? Wouldn't their brain already feel tired at the thought of the former and assume that a lot might be missing from the latter?

And they haven't even started reading.

So, let's assume that the length and title are lovely or that we can put those pre-judgements away.

The First Ten Pages

We might love or hate a script by page one. On the first page, we can learn a lot about the writing, style, genre, characters, professionalism, and the story's world. But a bit of time is often needed to set up a story, so we must put our judgements aside and keep going.

Ideally, we want to get interested by page 5. What if that doesn't happen?

This could occur for a myriad of reasons: talent (on the part of the writer), content, characters, and everything else we've talked about so far in this book. But still, we keep reading. Soon we will hit the first mark that is a big litmus test — the *inciting incident*. The belief in the industry is that by page ten something needs to happen. By "happen" I mean an action, a plot point, or event. The writer must dazzle us with their wordsmithery, have witty repartee between characters, or set up a delightful and original world. But by page 10 we need something to shake up the world and protagonist. It needs to get things in motion, and hint or even tell us, what the main plot will be. By page ten we need an event that propels the protagonist into the main action of the story.

Some examples:

> *Saving Private Ryan:* The death of the three Ryan Brothers is the inciting incident for General Marshall to find the last Ryan brother. A mother can't lose all her sons.
>
> *Jaws:* A woman is found dead. Before that, the town was normal. Now there's something afoot (or a-fin).
>
> *Hunger Games:* Katniss' sister is chosen, and Katniss chooses to take her place. She's changing things and making a sacrifice by enlisting in this hellish competition.
>
> *Harry Potter and the Philosopher's Stone:* Hagrid shows up and tells Harry that he's a wizard. Before this, he was an ordinary boy with a crappy life and cupboard.

The ordinary world alters. There's a change in the status quo, or a call to action, even if it's something seemingly innocuous like "I must have that girl." Something has changed and woken up the protagonist — or at least nudged them. We get a sense of where the story will *actively* take us. The main character may not yet have embarked on a new quest or action, but we know they will have to. For a bit of time, they can deny their destiny, plan, prepare, or try to stay stagnant, but ultimately they'll have to move forward.

If the script doesn't move things and move us by this point, some executives may give up, some Readers may shut down, and some audience members may feel bored or impatient. This is why we look for and rate an inciting incident by page ten. If it comes a little later, that could indicate that there's too much preamble, the writing is repetitive, or the pacing feels slow. A good inciting incident, occurring when it should, affects us emotionally, whether we're aware of it or not.

Protagonists Propelling Us out of Act One and into Act Two

The next thing we look for is that by the end of Act One (usually around pages 25-30 in a script 90-120 pages long), is that the protagonist is actively driving the plot and propelling us into the next act by pursuing a high stakes goal and battling very large antagonists and obstacles.

All those words are important.

1. The *protagonist* must be driving the plot, not others. This seems easy to spot, but not always. Imagine that parents send a shy kid

to summer camp to become more social. It is the parents who have the goals and desires whereas the protagonist is just a vehicle, reacting and responding. It would be different if the parents sent the kid to camp and, by the end of Act One, the kid decided to escape, lose their virginity, take the camp over, etc. Then *the kid* has the goal.

2.   The goal must have *high stakes*. The enemy will destroy the planet, the kid has to get into *that college*, the person is obsessed with *that girl*, promotion, or prize. This means that a bit of Act One must be spent showing us why the stakes matter. As a Reader, I might not want to be the biggest Instagram influencer, but if I understand what it means in that character's world, to their sense of self and happiness, I'll go along. In other words, we must identify with something about their goal. The protagonist's initial goal should evolve, but in the beginning we must believe that they *must* achieve it. Charlie Babbit must use his brother to get money in *Rainman* even though by the end, he would rather have his brother and love instead of money.

3.   They must battle a powerful *antagonist or obstacle*. By the end of Act One we should also know of any obstacles, conflicts, and antagonists. It's not enough for Romeo to love Juliet, we must know that their families are enemies. These can't be small obstacles or antagonists. For Readers and audiences to become invested, we need to know that the mission will not be easy. This is the part of the roller coaster ride where we're lifting our arms and giving caution to the wind but we have trepidation because we know there are obstacles and scary twists and turns ahead.

How the Heck to Keep Things Escalating for 60 Pages (Act Two)

Act Two is a beast. It usually runs from about pages 30-90. How does a script keep things moving for that long? Somehow the protagonist must keep driving events, as the stakes, conflicts, obstacles, and story continue to escalate. And that's what we, as Readers, look for.

It's not a coincidence that, when outlining the second act, some of my students find themselves despairing, lost, uncertain and off-course. That's exactly how the protagonist feels.

It's a delicate dance between throwing larger and larger fires for the protagonist to put out (making them reactive) versus having them continually drive events while battling escalating obstacles in the pursuit of a high stakes goal (active). A reactive protagonist can make a script episodic: meaning that as each situation occurs, it's handled and then we move on until another situation arises. An episode of TV can introduce and resolve a story and be over, but in a feature film we want it to continue to escalate, and not start and stop, which will make it feel episodic.

This is a big issue with road trip movies. The characters are in Iowa fighting the biggest ball of twine in the world and then it's over. They drive on… Then they encounter a love interest, get and lose her in Wyoming, then that's over. They drive on…

Readers must ask: Is the goal big enough, and is the protagonist focused enough on obtaining it? Are they knocking down larger and larger things *in pursuit of that goal*? Often a character wants something but then spends 12 pages hanging out at a bonfire, learning about life, and then gets back to their goal. This causes a gap in escalation, makes the audience/reader wonder if the goal was that important in the first place, slows down momentum, and adds to an episodic nature. Not to say that breaks never occur, but the breaks need to be short — and part of the plan.

If a sheriff is chasing an outlaw, he can and should bed down for the night, and it's a great time for character development, but it must be brief, it must have some incident(s) that heighten stakes or conflict (he hurts his shooting arm), and/or reveal some deeper or higher stakes (the outlaw killed the sheriff's mama). Or maybe he gives a young kid shooting lessons (with his eye on the goal, this is possibly a set up that the kid will help out later).

The point is that all scenes and sequences need to keep the story moving and heighten or deepen stakes and conflicts.

Mapping Act Two

One thing I always advise is for the writer to give the protagonist a map (literal or metaphorical) or steps to their plan so that by the end of Act One, they (and we) know what they're going to do. Then we can track and measure their success through Act Two. This also helps make the actions in Act Two not feel random.

For example, at the end of Act One a treasure hunter can tell their crew that they need to sail to Litterbox Island, buy ten magic kittens, then go to Cat Lady Island, trade the cats for fuel, get through the windy storms around the Nip of Great Hope, fight the Dog people of Bark Mountain to get to the top of Mount Fire Hydrant where the golden leash of Lassie-gula is… The point is, if we go through Act Two knowing beforehand how each action leads to the next one and all of them lead to the final goal, it won't feel like a bunch of episodes. It also helps to have a very personal life-and-death stake to get the goal, as opposed to just riches. Perhaps the golden leash will quell the dog riots back home, win them the woman they love's hand in marriage, or get them out of crippling debt. The leash isn't just a valuable prize, it serves a larger and more personal purpose.

Establishing Goals and Tracking Success

It's also important to track the character's progress or, with a more intangible goal such as love or acceptance, find a way to measure if they've achieved it or not. Perhaps a kid wants to be popular. How will we know when they achieve popularity? We can measure their success at this goal by various milestones: losing their virginity, being crowned Prom King, or getting two million followers on social media.

A second act needs to keep the goal present, heighten and deepen conflicts and relationships, ensure the protagonist has a plan we can track and measure, and escalate the obstacles.

Here are a few other tips to use and items to look for:

- **Do mysteries unravel?** These are trackable questions that are planted early, get revealed little by little, and keep our interest.
- **Interweave subplots that follow their own structure.** Subplots add layers and inform and/or provide breaks from the main plot. They should also have a character driving them with their personal obstacles, beginnings, middles, ends, and arcs.
- **Is there a "ticking clock?"** Do they have a week to get 11,000 votes to be Prom King? The shorter the time, the higher the tension.
- **And finally, do we track the character's arc?** It's good to see the protagonist grow and change, but not too much — yet.

For an internal arc, a character has had a flaw, been blind to see something about themselves, or aren't fully embracing who they are. By the midpoint, they either have a crack and start to change or get a real glimpse of a different way of being but ignore it. They should keep resisting so it gets them to...

The Nudge They Ignore or Crack That Just Begins

In most love triangle movies, the hero may like the wrong person for the wrong reasons, and by the resolution end up with the right person for the right reasons. The right person may have been there all along but they needed to change. By the midpoint they may notice something bad about the wrong person or good about the right person, but shake it off. Perhaps Archie likes rich girl Veronica, but Betty is truly right for him. By the midpoint, maybe Veronica stands him up, or Betty does something sweet. There's a moment where Archie may have a jolt to his feelings, but he doesn't change yet. He still goes for the wrong girl, and usually for the wrong reasons. A crack has pierced his armor but he ignored it, hasn't learned his lesson or transformed enough to see what he truly needs. And that leads to…

It All Comes Crashing Down — Externally and Internally (End of Act Two)

This is where the ride sucks everything out of us. In fact, it's great if the ride breaks down and the audience feels that they're going to die (in the metaphor of a script's structure). In a screenplay of about 110-120 pages or so, this often occurs around page 90.

The main point is that all must seem lost to the protagonist or ensemble, and to the audience. Externally and internally. As we were told in film school: "Throw a cat up a tree, throw rocks at it and set the tree on fire."

Don't Save the Protagonist (Yet)

Though in life we want safety, writers must battle that desire and put their characters in extreme jeopardy. Often, perhaps subconsciously, writers make it too easy or they may throw in tiny rays of hope before the end of Act Two. But they shouldn't.

For example, a character has an eviction notice but we've already cut to a scene of their dad sending them money for Christmas.

This is the writer signaling that help is on the way, but they shouldn't do this. The cat needs to be up a tree, the rocks are hurling, and the fire is raging. Don't establish a catnip-encrusted rock-catcher and fire hose beside them.

Readers, when doing coverage and assessing structure in Act Two, look to see that the writer has successfully done the following:

> Do obstacles heighten and yet the protagonist keeps driving things?
> Does the plot keep escalating?
> Can we track the character's arc?
> Can we measure their steps or plans?
> Is there a crack at the midpoint?
> Are there interweaving subplots?
> And does all seem hopelessly and absolutely lost by the end of it?

The Protagonist Better Change to Pull Off Act Three

Act Three is supposed to be the biggest, most active act of all. Just when all seems lost, the characters must grow, take huge risks, sacrifice, change, and then fight their biggest battle.

Transformation

In the end of *Rainman*, Charlie finally prioritizes his brother and treats his girlfriend better. This helps us track how he's grown. He even sacrifices the money he's been chasing. Protagonists often give up their initial goal for something bigger or better. In doing so, they obtain their true goal (because they made a sacrifice or change) or they might get what they *need* instead. Charlie wanted his father's money and got a relationship with his brother instead.

If the protagonist has been a jerk to women, maybe they become nicer. If they had to lead a group of people but ignored other characters' advice, maybe now they listen. If they achieved popularity but lost all their real friends, maybe they must give up the Prom King crown to make amends since they now realize what's truly important.

Whatever the change, it will lead to…

Taking Risks

Externally and internally, the protagonist must get up, thoroughly and totally wounded, and keep going. They lost the treasure but they go on… for love. They'll risk their reputation to tell the truth. They go back to people they've hurt and make amends. They stop being selfish. They do this because they must, in Act Three, fight their…

Biggest Battles

The final battle must be *massive*, internally and externally. Did the writer do a good job establishing what the stakes are? Is the antagonist or obstacle so formidable that we're still crapping our pants for them to face it?

This battle can't be the same level as previous ones. It needs to be the Mama of all battles. And battles don't need to look like all 46 Avengers battling Thanos. It can look like a kid coming out to his parents or someone telling a love interest how they feel. It can be making amends to all the people a character scorched. But achieving this should take *everything* the character has. What's more, it should be obvious that they couldn't have won this battle in the beginning because they weren't capable of it then.

So make sure the writer plants, tracks, and pays those elements off.

❓ A, B, and C Storylines

In screenwriting, the main story is known as the *A plot* or *A story*. The most important subplot is the *B plot*, followed by the *C plot* and so on. These subplots add more layers, levels and texture. Identifying storylines can help Readers determine whether or not the structure of a film is working.

Subplots

Another aspect of story structure is the tracking, relevance, and structure of subplots.

- **We can track the main character's secondary goals.** If May's A plot is to develop the technology to send a shuttle to Mars, she may also have a B plot or goal, such as dealing with a loved one's deteriorating memory.
- **We track secondary characters and their B plot goals**, such as — while May develops the technology to send a shuttle to Mars (A plot), her sister runs for Congress against a powerful incumbent (B plot).
- **We track things in the world, environment, community, society,** etc. While May develops the technology to send a shuttle to Mars, space debris is about to hit Indiana.

The point of subplots is that they give us a break from the main plot, and in the best cases, help, hinder, heighten, or inform the main plot. They also help keep Act Two interesting, escalating, and moving forward.

Non-Subpar Subplots

For Readers and writers, here are a few items to look for in a well-crafted subplot:

> **First, does it interweave with the A plot?** As stated, subplots often give us a break from the main plot, but development of a subplot should be interspersed throughout and structured the same as an A plot (inciting incident, end of Act One active goal…)
>
> **Is it active and character-driven?** Does the subplot have a protagonist that pursues a goal, battles conflicts, and causes a

resolution? The best ones do. For example, if May's sister runs for Congress, in Act One she goes for it, in Act Two there are complications and escalations as she fights the incumbent, and by the end of Act Two she should hit her lowest point. Then in Act Three she will fight her most active battle, hopefully having an internal change or arc of her own as well.

Does the subplot track? Is there a beginning, middle and end to the subplot?

Does the subplot thematically parallel or contrast to the main story? The best ones do. Better than following an A plot about Ro's music career with an unrelated subplot about a whale in captivity, it would be great if somehow the plots related or at least thematically related or contrasted.

ℹ Runners

Short for *running jokes,* runners consist of a recurring element that intensifies due to repetition. For example, there might be a stoner friend we check on from time to time, or a funny dog who's always stealing food. These can give comic relief, or even in serious scripts, can highlight or add levels, symbolism, and color. Perhaps we track the autumn leaves falling as someone battles a crippling disease.

What to Watch: *Seinfeld*

One show with an advanced example of interweaving subplots is the TV Show, *Seinfeld.* At its best, (after season 2) it would establish an A, B, C and D plot, track and interweave them, and then usually, based on the characters' selfishness, all stories would intersect, and no one would obtain their goal thanks to the other characters and plots. It was a heck of a thing to see. Its stepdaughter, *Curb Your Enthusiasm,* has a slightly similar structure. Each episode sets up multiple plots and subplots that all come together — and usually kick the protagonist in the butt. Most other shows have *parallel plots* and subplots that intersect but not always.

Studying Structure: *Hidden Figures*

Hidden Figures is an interesting film to look at for structure. There are three interweaving plots which, based on screen time given, can be delineated into A, B and C plots, as well as runners, and each one tracks with a beginning, middle and an end. When I had one of the writers, Allison Schroeder, speak to my class, she said she outlined each of the stories separately and then wove them together. That's a good idea and something I do as well. What is my beginning, middle, and end for each story, and then where do I place them (using index cards, a dry erase board, Final Draft's storyboard feature, etc.) so that they each track in respect to their own stories, and to the structure as a whole?

So, when reading a script, look to see if the subplots' stories track — beginning, middle and end — and if they are spaced out and consistently interweave with the main plot. For example, it would feel off if they didn't start the B plot till Act Two, followed it for 15 pages and then it disappeared. We want to establish all subplots by the end of Act One, track them in Act Two, and resolve them in Act Three.

No One Just Gets Lucky!

A final note for the structure category is something I alluded to before: Don't have "lucky" characters. We want them to work hard, initiate action, and earn what they get. Look out for the deadly…

Passive Protagonists, Random Helpers, and Contrived Situations — Oh My!

Contrived and *coincidental* are words I often use to describe characters and elements that I can tell the writer needed to bring in to help resolve a conflict, but weren't first set up and then paid off, or caused/earned by the main characters. They just were thrown in and the character got lucky. For example, a character is about to be killed and a streetlamp "happens" to fall and knock out the assailant. Look out for those.

As I've mentioned, there are characters who need to learn to take control of their lives and chart their own courses, but overall, we don't want things thrown to or at them, making them too passive or reactive. Watch out for people "tripping over" or "luckily" finding the magic coin, gun, or wisdom they just happened to need right at that moment. We also don't want helpers and allies who weren't set up but then appear exactly when needed.

When a Script Feels Episodic

As I mentioned before, getting into a situation, completing it, and moving on to the next can make a script feel episodic, as do things happening *to* — rather than *by* — the main character. We want characters earning their tragedies and victories, and for the plot to continually escalate and not start and stop.

Building an Arc

We talked about character arcs in Chapter 6, but arcs can also be associated with structure. Do events happen gradually and organically, over the three acts? Can we get inside the characters and understand how, why, and when they change? Too often I've seen a relationship or character arc complete way too early, all at once in a rush at the end, or not at all.

Basically:

Have a character flawed in Act One, something starts to crack by the midpoint, have all seem lost by the end of Act Two when they still haven't changed, and then let them slowly rise up, grow, change, sacrifice, and with this newfound knowledge or way of being, fight their biggest internal and external battles in Act Three to come out the other side, somehow transformed in the end (Figure 8.1).

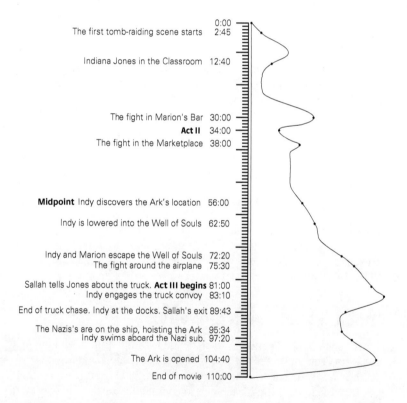

The first tomb-raiding scene starts	0:00 / 2:45
Indiana Jones in the Classroom	12:40
The fight in Marion's Bar	30:00
Act II	34:00
The fight in the Marketplace	38:00
Midpoint Indy discovers the Ark's location	56:00
Indy is lowered into the Well of Souls	62:50
Indy and Marion escape the Well of Souls	72:20
The fight around the airplane	75:30
Sallah tells Jones about the truck. **Act III begins**	81:00
Indy engages the truck convoy	83:10
End of truck chase. Indy at the docks. Sallah's exit	89:43
The Nazis's are on the ship, hoisting the Ark	95:34
Indy swims aboard the Nazi sub.	97:20
The Ark is opened	104:40
End of movie	110:00

Figure 8.1

This diagram shows the story structure of *Raiders of the Lost Ark*, a classic example of three-act structure for feature films.

"I Gotta Be Me. Formulas Stifle Me!"

I'll say it again: these are guidelines, not formulas. I don't want to ruin what someone wants to say in their screenplay by dictating rigid rules for how to say it. There *are* reasons for the guidelines, mainly because they help with pacing, emotional investment, drama, and tension. But rules can be broken once a writer knows how or are already successful and well-known.

Exercises

Here are three scenes towards the end of a screenplay. Come up with two possible setups for each, to help towards a resolution.

For example, if I have girl scouts on a trip, stuck in a cave with a bear about to eat them, perhaps I had earlier set up that one girl was amazing at archery and strangely brought a bow and arrow with her wherever she went. Now she can use it to scare — not kill- the bear (it's a G rated family film).

1. The two men were upstairs, and I was in the basement. I could hear them arguing through the vent. The bigger one was saying it was over; they were going to kill me. I tried to move, to scream, but I was handcuffed to a pole, and gagged.

2. That was it. I'd lost the school election. The votes had been counted and my sister had won by four.

3. I ran and ran- I had to stop the wedding. I had let my pride get in the way and would not let it anymore! I leaped out of my Uber to the wedding but it was too late—I stopped in my tracks. There she was, with him, leaving the church- officially married, the well-wishing guests throwing rice on them.

9

Dialogue

Look Who's Talking

Anyone who has ever tried to talk to someone they're romantically interested in but accidentally spurted out: "Do you like bread?! I very much like bread!" and then heard crickets and silence, knows very well about the importance of dialogue.

In theatrical plays, dialogue can go on longer than it does in cinema. Plays tend to focus more on the characters, dialogue, and on fewer situations. A 14-page scene in a play that's mostly conversational is not considered a problem. Parents who need to tell their kid they're adopted can make small talk and build up to it for 13 pages.

Not so in a movie or TV script.

Movie and TV series dialogue is not the same as regular spoken language. Unless we're in a Woody Allen movie, film dialogue usually doesn't have all the "um's," hesitancies, and strange ticks.

Screenplay dialogue is a stylized form, often capturing the essence — not the realities — of regular speech.

For example, we don't write this:

```
                    Lara
          Excuse me?


                    Anton
          Yes?


                    Lara
          Wait. What was I thinking? Um… Um…
          Wait… Um…


                    Anton
              …


                    Lara
          Hold on. I know it was that thing….
          That… thing… that…
```

Rather, we write this:

```
                    Lara
          Hey. I forgot what I came to this
          store for, but now, in the presence
          of your dazzling brown eyes, I know
          what I need.


                    Anton
          Hubba hubba.
```

We skip the mess. *Less is more* and if a screenwriter can capture the voice, keep the story moving, make it interesting yet nuanced, inform the plot, and yet not hit us on the head with loads of information, then it works. Easy peasy.

One of my all-time favorite examples is this brief, effective dialogue exchange from *Escape from Alcatraz*:

```
                Charlie Butts
          What was your childhood like?


                Frank Morris
          Short.
```

That's clear, concise, and intriguing. And though dialogue is where the characters tell us things, the best dialogue *shows*, rather than *tells* us point blank who they are and how they see the world.

Stay Consistent

Like everything else in a screenplay, avoid inconsistencies in logic within the dialogue. Don't have a character say, "I moved here 17 years ago," and then say, "Yep. 45 years ago, when I first moved here."

Clear Voices

Characters should have distinct ways of speaking. The dialogue/voice should inform who they are. Characterization comes from action, behavior, arcs, and relationships, but also in what they say and often what they *don't* say. A character saying that their childhood was "short" tells a lot. And the fact that the character says nothing else, tells us even more.

Just like real people, some characters blather and some think before they speak. Some say what they feel, and many do not.

Bad example of two people on a first date at a restaurant:

                    Jovan
          I am a person.

                    Michelle
          I too am a person.

Better example:

                    Michael
          I want kids. Beautiful, healthy,
          amazing, and adorable kids.
          Multitudes. Scores. Tens of
          thousands. Oh, their adoring faces
          and exquisite minds…

                    Henry
          I want lasagna.

The audience doesn't want to do a lot of work, but they want to do some. They can infer a lot from an exchange like that. We get a sense of each person and of how they might or might not be suited to each other. In just two lines.

As the above example in the restaurant depicts, the voices should also be distinctive from each other. Now, I'm not saying that five Frat Bro's wouldn't sound similar, but a common error and source of frustration is when they all sound exactly the same and the Reader gets confused and can't keep track of them. And naming them SKINNY BRO', HEAVY BRO' IN TANK TOP, BRO' WITH TOWEL AROUND HIS WAIST, and STONED BRO' doesn't fix it.

Look at how hard this would be to follow:

          Five teens hang out under the bleachers.

                    Kid 1
          Pass the joint.

```
            Kid 2
      This rocks.


            Kid 3
      Did you do the homework?


            Kid 4
      I didn't.


            Kid 5
      What time is it?


            Kid 2
      11:40.


            Kid 4
      Cool, lunch is next.


            Kid 4
      Not for me. I got lunch 6ᵗʰ period...
```

Yes, we can give names, action, behavior, and a little qualifier, but distinctive voices are critical. Such as:

```
            Kid 1
      Damn, I need some sweet sweet kush.
      Who's holding?


            Kid 2
      Nah, man. That's the Devil's tool
      used by the government to control
      our minds.


            Kid 3
      Chan eil Beurla agam.


            Kid 4
      God, I hate the new Scottish Gaelic
      kid. WHAT ARE YOU SAYING? Man, I'm
      always angry!


            Kid 5
      Help. I have been stuck under these
      bleachers for 250 years by an
      ancient Golem, and if you free me,
      I'll grant you three wishes!
```

See? A nice, cohesive scene that we might see in a coming-of-age movie, with unique voices for each character.

Look at a movie like Hidden Figures: all three women are African American, smart, and oppressed (both within America and in their jobs at NASA) but their different attitudes, characters, and POV come out both in action and dialogue. Also, it's not just what the characters say — sometimes we learn a lot from what others say about them.

Imagine someone comes into a room and asks, "Is this seat taken" and four people all say, "Yes, it is!" Then that person stands awkwardly, sweats profusely, and moves on. One of the other people can put their bag on the chair and say, "God, she's so awkward and irritating. I thought she'd never leave." Now this tells us a lot about that "awkward" person, but we also might not have seen enough from them. We don't know if that person is actually irritating or if those people are overreacting, mean, or judgmental. So, dialogue can help — but we must also see the behavior to learn more about the character and understand how we're supposed to perceive them.

Earning What Is Said About Them

What one character says about another can give us a lot of information, but (and I give this note a lot) the character must earn what's said about them. We can't just be told how they are; we have to see it. For example, we don't want a normal character that someone says is "painfully, excruciatingly shy," but then never see them act that way.

Appropriate to Time, Location, and World

Whether it's a period piece, another world, a different culture, region, society, age, or point of view, the dialogue must reflect that milieu and stay consistent. This may seem obvious, but there are subtle ways this rule gets broken. Yes, someone asking for a cell phone in the year 1650 is an easy one to spot, but that's not always the case.

There are different terms, cadences, patterns, slang, levels, and so on if characters are:

- Giving a keynote speech at a conference on quantum physics and the nature of computation.
- Rallying a small militia for the Revolutionary War.
- At a high school in an inner city.
- At a high school in a wealthy community.
- Planning the conquest of the Boopboop Galaxy and preparing to battle the great Prawn Mice Warriors.
- Texting on Grindr.
- Being heartfelt and authentic.
- Being "woke."

Rules for how each character speaks must be established and then their dialogue must stay consistent with those rules. For example, if the aliens on a planet speak like Earth's 1980's Valley girls, so be it. However, once this is established, it's important to keep it that way.

The show *Deadwood* had amazing language from the 1800s — it was almost Shakespearean in its complexities and poetic nature. However, it amazed me that every single character constantly used the word "c-ksucker." It was odd when a Chinese man who basically spoke no English seemed to know that one word. I wasn't aware if this was a common term at the time, but eventually I accepted it. These were the rules the writers established and by gum, they stuck to them.

Subtext

Most satisfying and compelling dialogue has two levels: what a character says and what they mean.

For example: Aunt Sadie pinches her nephew Ryan's' cheek with an iron grip. When Ryan's mother instructs him to tell Aunt Sadie that he loves her, he might say those words: "I love you, Aunt Sadie". But his watery eyes, red face, and buckling knees indicate something else.

While there are exceptions, in modern society people don't always say what they mean, or they may have undertones to what they're saying. We can argue about whether or not that is true in the real world, but in good screenwriting, subtext is quite essential.

Here's some dialogue for a romantic scene with no subtext:

```
          Corey
Hi.

          Stacy
Hi.

          Corey
You're cute and I've liked you for
a while.

          Stacy
Thank you. I think you are cute,
and I also have liked you for a
while.

          Corey
Let's date.

          Stacy
We simply must.
```

We don't want to make the audience to work too hard to understand what the characters mean when they speak but we do want them to invest, infer, and discover who people are through their words. For example, when it comes to dating, some people and characters have impressive game. They can go up to someone in a bar and say, "I like you. Can I have your number?" That simple exchange conveys a clear, direct, and confident character.

True story: I once did go to a bar (when we still did that). I was petrified but pushed through to someone and said, "I think you're attractive. (Beat) Okay, now I have to run away."

That interchange conveys a very different character. If that were in a script, we'd know a lot about my character and become more invested. Hopefully a Reader could feel my anxiety.

Should There Always Be Subtext?

Not always, so Readers shouldn't just jump on all direct and blatant dialogue. There are exceptions, for example often in period pieces characters speak more directly, especially during climactic or emotional moments — such as a war scene. Readers will also find those huge, inspiring, vulnerable, or risk-taking monologues that come at pivotal moments and aren't the norm for films set in modern times. *A Few Good Men* doesn't open with the "You Can't Handle the Truth" speech — a character is pushed to it.

Here's a taste:

```
          Colonel Nathan R. Jessup
You can't handle the truth! Son, we
live in a world that has walls, and
those walls have to be guarded by
men with guns. Who's gonna do it?
You? You, Lieutenant Weinberg? I
have a greater responsibility than
you can possibly fathom. You weep
for Santiago, and you curse the
Marines. You have that luxury. You
have the luxury of not knowing what
I know -- that Santiago's death,
while tragic, probably saved lives;
and my existence, while grotesque
and incomprehensible to you, saves
lives…
```

If we use enough subtext and layered dialogue, it helps frame important moments like these when characters finally reveal "their truth" (which of course, we supposedly can't handle).

On-The-Nose Exposition

There shouldn't be too much information or exposition crammed into the dialogue all at once. While writers need to get some information out, they must do that subtly as well. Audiences want to be shown who people, situations, relationships, stories, conflicts, goals, stakes, and worlds are — rather than be told or "hit on the head" with information. In fact, a common term for overdoing it and having characters hammer us with information is that the dialogue is *on the nose*.

Instead of "We are brothers" a character can approach someone and say, "Mom says for you to come home." Simple differences like "my mom" versus "mom" convey a lot.

More is More?

In coverage, I also note if characters need to give *more* information. I'll write a comment such as, "The characters may understand their internal references, but the audience might need more help."

For example, if one friend says to another, "I finally did it!" That's normal and sounds natural, but we might not understand what they're referring to. People who know each other often have a shorthand when talking but the audience will need more information.

Similarly, real-life brothers wouldn't say: "This land we have grown up on has been good. The soil has been good. The trees have been strong, and that shed has been here for generations." But they also need to do more than just look around and say, "This is good." There should be a happy medium. Perhaps something like: "After twenty years, you're going to just leave the farm? After all that it's given to us — and what it's cost mom and dad in toil and sacrifice? WTF, Jebediah?"

Too Technical

Overly technical dialogue doesn't just refer to scientific people talking in scientific terms. Many characters use terms and jargon that is the norm for their environment, characters, situation, or group but that a "civilian" audience might not understand. I often find myself looking up terms used by people in the Enlightenment, or by gamers, younger people, airline workers, and tech bros. They all have their own language and viewers will need help to understand it.

When Tech Talk Works

The NASA characters in *Hidden Figures* and the crew in *The Big Bang Theory* spout a lot of terminology but we're not meant to get the actual content. The dialogue is there to establish that these characters are knowledgeable, that something big is happening, or it conveys their intelligence.

For example, we can use complex dialogue to inform character, a relationship, or a situation:

```
              Wendy
I want to prove that at the heart
of every black hole must be a point
where space and time themselves
break down — a singularity.


              Pierre
I want lasagna.
```

In this case, the jargon could be a set up for a joke or maybe it's intended to depict differences between two characters. The audience doesn't need to understand the complexities of that first sentence in order to understand the scene.

But if dialogue contains something that viewers need to know to understand the scene, the tech talk should be simplified or framed so that it's understandable. Again, it should be done subtly, avoiding "on the nose" exposition. And when possible, it should also be brief and interesting.

Repetition

Dialogue shouldn't be repetitive. If we're being hit over the head by a point that's already been made or different characters offer the same information, the plot isn't escalating.

A writer may be blind to repetitive dialogue, but Readers, executives, and audiences can feel when a point has been made too many times. A script shouldn't have six different people telling a character they need new shoes or a partner saying, "You're annoying!" more than once without it escalating. And by escalating, I mean that each time something is heightened — such as the incident (they get more annoying) or the reaction (the partner gets more and more annoyed) as a build up to a huge pay off.

❓ The Rule of Threes

The comedy *rule of threes* is a writing principle that suggests that a trio of events or characters is more humorous, satisfying, or effective than other numbers.

Indulgent Dialogue

A final problem to look for is dialogue that rambles on and on, usually for one of the following reasons:

- **A writer is in love with their own writing.** Therefore, they go on and on, because they're having such a great time.
- **It's a comedy and they have to throw in more jokes.** While this technique is good to keep the funny going, it's not good when it's at the expense of plot and pace.
- **The writer doesn't trust themselves or the audience** so they tend to over-explain.
- **They've researched the heck out of a time period**, subject, world, or whatnot and want to use what they've learned.
- **They're well-versed in a subject or terminology** and write everything exactly as *they'd* say it.
- **They respond in witty or smart dialogue** instead of action, emotion, or a strong reaction. They write what they think someone would *say* in a situation, when it really calls for a reaction, action, or even silence.

For example, many of us might deflect a serious or painful situation with humor and so might a character, but if it happens at the expense of drama, it may be that *the writer* doesn't want to delve or deal with deeper issues.

Exercises

Sometimes the best way to understand scripts is to try a little writing yourself. In the exercises below, I will introduce a situation, type of characters, world or time period. Write a dialogue exchange between two characters but remember to make the two people distinctive from each other and appropriate to time and place. Give enough information but not too much, use subtext and move the plot forward. There should also be some conflict, not just two people agreeing with each other.

1. Two ancient Greek or Roman soldiers argue about who will be made general.

2. A breakup where one person does not expect it.

3. A gamer takes their grandfather to a huge gaming exposition.

And for a bonus, take the two characters you came up with from Chapter 6 (Character) and write them in one of the above scenarios.

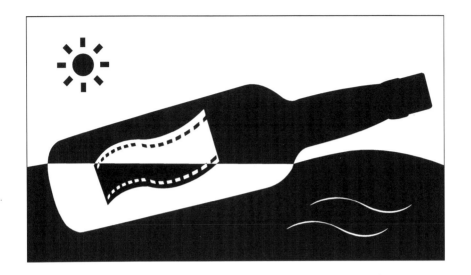

10

Theme

But What About Fart Joke Movies?

Everything Has a Message

Every film, show, story, poem, person, and experience are chock-full of lessons, even simple ones. My cat provides lessons just by crunching on dry food after a few teeth have been pulled and I think, "He's not complaining about how much easier it would be if he still had all his teeth. He's just figuring out how to adapt and eat. He doesn't dwell on what isn't. He just deals with what is."

If I can get deep lessons from my cat and his kibble, then audiences can get lessons from a hot tub time travel movie, a quest for a dude to get his car, a group of friends hungover after a night in Vegas, or three kids dealing with sex toys and drugs as they try to get a drone back.

Themes can be found if we look, and they often add heart to humor, layers and nuance to make the two-or-so hour movie experience even more valuable, and help the audience emotionally invest more.

Not every script leans heavily on a theme or attempts to transform our world view. Some offer humor or escape. But not only can one still find themes in those lighter fares, but as Readers, we often have to.

As the sample coverage templates show, often there are categories where we're asked to rate and comment on the themes of the script. And while we can claim that themes don't shout at us because it's not "that kind of film," they still need to be stated.

Therefore, themes and messages are another element to look for when assessing a screenplay. Some companies specifically want "deeper fare," especially those that produce more complex and nuanced films, or agents who represent people who want to direct or star in complex and nuanced roles.

Showing vs. Telling

I find myself writing the same note over and over in coverage: that themes and messages are told to us too literally, whether in dialogue or with too much narration or voice-over. Voicing themes is great for shows like *Doogie Howser*: "That's when I learned that taking out a spleen might be easier than taking out a girl..." Or the original *Wonder Years*: "Why did my sister burn her bra? What a waste. I could've used it to practice unhooking them." But those series actually taught lessons every week and set up devices to convey them, such as Doogie's ancient computer diary, or Fred Savage's bouncing eyebrows.

In some scripts it feels like the writer teaches or preaches their message to us — making sure we don't miss *the big lesson* — which can overwhelm the plot or a character's journey. Lessons must be shown but audiences should *discover them for themselves, through experience.* Actions, consequences, arcs, and reactions of the characters — through these devices, audiences learn what the characters learn.

Some of the best messages and themes are conveyed by how love interests, buddies, or partners *affect each other*. A love interest can help someone open up, trust, or embrace parts of themselves. Buddies can inspire one another to grieve, speak up, or get out of their comfort zones. Coworkers and partners can encourage peers to go for their dream, do what's right, buck the system, etc.

Humor can also help convey themes — since "a spoonful of sugar helps the medicine go down." Oh yeah, songs also convey themes. For example, the movie *Superbad* is more than a coming-of-age, penis joke movie, because it's based on something deeper: how close Seth and Evan are, how threatened Seth feels by that relationship changing, and how scared he is of losing Evan's friendship. There's a hell of a lot of (humor) sugar, but the (heart) medicine grounds it.

Hitting Us Over the Head

As a Readers, we develop a sense of when a *writer tells* the message rather than having characters experience it so that we can infer and discover it for ourselves. Sometimes the message is conveyed well, but then conveyed again and again. We can almost hear the writer saying, "But do they get it? Do they really? Maybe I should make the point one — or ten — more times."

As Readers we can point out how much is too much.

For example, just as comedy comes in threes, so can themes if they escalate in set-ups, complications, and pay offs. Perhaps a character is prejudiced and misses one opportunity — but doesn't learn. Then misses another and considers a new way of thinking — but still doesn't learn or change. And in the end, they either finally change — or don't and suffer the tragic consequences. That works.

Themes from Characters — Building an Arc

No matter how overt or subtle, themes are best conveyed through the characters' experiences, emotional journeys, what they learn, how they relate to others, and how the experience changes them.

The categories of theme, character, and structure all intersect in this Venn Diagram of a point:

One of the best ways to convey theme is if a character has a flaw, blind spot, or a lesson to learn but doesn't learn it. Then all heck breaks loose and they finally must transform — or suffer the consequences. And the arc must track — meaning we must see how the characters were, how they started to think or feel differently, and then, in the end, how they've transformed.

Thematic Titles

Titles can help convey a message, but hopefully don't bludgeon us. *Dear White People* is a great and subtle title that conveys the series' theme. *"I Hate Being at This Racist School and We're Going to Tell You About it from Different Points of View"* would be less subtle.

As Readers, when we're figuring out the theme of a script, we can look in various places:

* The title. (*Love Conquers All.*)

- What a character learns or how they change. (In the end, Ronald understood that love conquers all.)
- Important speeches. (Ronald: "Love conquers all, y'all!")

And in many other elements, such as setting, cultures, relationships, etc.

- *Star Trek* taught about unity through their peace-keeping missions.
- *Straight Outta Compton* showed us many examples of systemic racism.
- *Lord of The Rings* teaches about courage, duty, loyalty, sacrifice and friendship.

We Get It. This Is a Very Important Movie

"Important" movies can really shake us up and that's incredible. I could barely sit through the scene in the movie *Ray* where the mother has to let her little blind son call out for her, cry, and bump around the little shack thinking he was all alone — all so he could become independent. They went deep and boy, did I get the message: sometimes one needs to use tough love in order to toughen someone up for life.

I once read a script where a young man was obsessed with an obscure politician. He named a business after him, spoke about him, and tried to get everyone to understand what was so important about him. I learned about the politician, but I didn't "get" his importance (for either the protagonist or for myself). The emotional connection — why that politician mattered so much to that character — wasn't there. I wanted less facts and more feeling. Show me how that politician fills a hole in the protagonist and inspires them to dream, improve, heal, or grow, and I'll get the message. If a writer wants to educate the world, go through our hearts and minds. As Readers, we can help them do this.

For example: In *Hidden Figures,* we don't need to be told that 1950's-60's NASA was racist. We watch Viola Davis rush to the restroom for Black people all the way across campus.

We don't need huge speeches — we watch Norma Rae hold up a "Union" sign and see the other characters' reactions. (*Norma Rae*)

We can watch two high school best buds, after a fight, drunkenly snuggle in a sleeping bag, confess their love, but then act like nothing happened the next morning as they both go to a mall and hang with girls. (*Superbad*)

Like with so many other aspects of a script, to convey a message, show us don't tell us.

Exercises

1. List 2-3 possible themes from:

   A. Your favorite comedy.

   B. A romantic drama.

   C. A huge epic film.

   How did you get the message? What specifically drove it home and did it do it well, or was it too subtle or too on the nose?

2. Come up with five themes (besides *love conquers all*) and for each one, think of (a made up) plot that could depict it.

3. What themes do you think would be depicted in the following films?

   > *The Artist:* Hollywood, 1927. As silent movie star George Valentin wonders if the arrival of talking pictures will cause him to fade into oblivion, he sparks with Peppy Miller, a young dancer set for a big break.
   >
   > *Bridges of Madison County:* An Iowa housewife, stuck in her routine, must choose between true romance and the needs of her family.
   >
   > *Django Unchained:* After being rescued by a German bounty hunter, a freed slave sets out to rescue his wife from a brutal Mississippi plantation owner.
   >
   > *Finding Nemo:* When his son is swept out to sea, an anxious clownfish embarks on a perilous journey across a treacherous ocean to bring him back.
   >
   > *Lean On Me:* A tough principal takes revolutionary measures to clean up a notoriously dangerous inner-city New Jersey high school.
   >
   > *Little Miss Sunshine:* When a wannabe child beauty queen learns that a spot has opened up in the "Little Miss Sunshine" pageant, she convinces her dysfunctional family to make the cross-country trek, despite her father's (and society's) protestations that she may not have what it takes to win.
   >
   > *The Sweet Smell of Success:* A press agent, hungry to get ahead, is pushed by a ruthless columnist to do cruel and evil things and is eventually caught in the web of lies that he has created.
   >
   > *Toy Story:* A cowboy doll is profoundly threatened and jealous when a new spaceman action figure supplants him as top toy in a boy's room.

Writer

Tone

Mood

Reader

11

Tone

Hilarious... Then Everyone Dies?

Tone — what is it? (Besides when a mother says, "Don't use that tone on me, young missy!")

It's the half sibling of style, a cousin-in-law once removed from genre, and three roads down and across the block from emotion. Got it? Good.

When we speak of the tone of a story, we're talking about a particular feeling conveyed by the writer. It can be joyful, serious, humorous, sad, threatening, formal, informal, pessimistic, optimistic, bleak, nostalgic, and so on.

While tone signifies a writer's point of view, the *mood* is the overall feeling that tone conveys to the *audience*. For example, my tone might be sarcastic, and the mood it evokes is dark and despairing. Often a tone may match the mood, such as writing something scary which leaves the audience, in fact, scared. But sometimes it's not. For example, if I write a scene where the audience knows that a bomb is hidden under a character's desk, but the character doesn't know, that scene can have a whimsical tone. Or I can write a scene showing a character ordering roses for a date, and imbue it with a suspenseful mood if I reveal something to the audience that the character doesn't know, such as the other person plans to break up that night.

Often, we might find short descriptions of films that convey the tone when perusing film streaming sites. For example, *Good on Paper*: "Deadpan. Raunchy. Irreverent."

Most company templates ask about tone for a few reasons. They want to know more than just the genre. They want to know what the audience may feel. What is the effect or mood? Is the mood clearly conveyed? Is it achieved effectively? Is it consistent? And again, some companies, agents, execs, networks, and platforms have tones they prefer.

Tone is something Readers must assess and report on, especially since a synopsis often tells what the story is about, but doesn't always convey the tone, mood, or effect.

Establishing the Tone Early

No matter the project, as quickly as possible, scripts need to inform the Reader/audience who, what, where they are, what to expect, and how things work. So too, with tone. Is the story to come a light one? Dark? Realistic? Surreal? Raw? Harsh? Unsettling?

For example, take the Netflix show, *Ratched*. The original film on which it's based, *One Flew Over the Cuckoo's Nest,* was (for 1975) gritty, edgy, slow, realistic, subtle, and deep. When I settled in to watch *Ratched*, I expected the same tone, but oh no, I was wrong. So very wrong.

As soon as *Ratched* began, I was transported into a world of melodrama (this was neither good nor bad, but it was not what I was prepared for). Events, dialogue, costumes, music, lighting, and color were all extremely prominent. Where much was subtle in the movie, in the TV series it was all neon and stylized.

Ratched is by Ryan Murphy, whose works always have a certain style and tone. He is even quoted as saying, "In TV tone is everything." He usually has a cinematic, glitzy style and tone, often combining melodrama, camp, the grotesque and so on. Sometimes it's more comic as in *Scream Queens*, or more serious-ish, as in *American Horror Story*. He can be soapy and over-the-top, such as with *Pose* and *Ratched,* but even shows like *Feud* or *The Politician* feel a bit stylized or hyper-real. *Glee* may have been his most down-to-earth project — but it was also a musical.

Now, consider the show, *The Handmaid's Tale*. Both the content and tone are quite harsh and bleak. I've heard quite a few people say they couldn't continue watching because it was so harsh — especially when the current times were bleak as well (politics, protests, pandemic, etc.) And, strangely enough, the tone of *Handmaid's Tale* gets quite nuanced and complex. The reality is unbearable but then Elizabeth Moss' voice-overs contrast and provide some dark humor. The same was true for *Dexter*. The voice-over added irreverence and humor to the dark subject matter. The contrast of voice-over to action altered and layered the tone of these shows.

Scripts should establish the tone right away, especially since some templates ask if the tone is clearly defined within the first 5-10 pages.

Messing with an Audience and Then Changing It Up on Them

Every good project can have a mixture of tones. For example, horror and action movies need a bit of romance, humor, or personal stories to give us a break from the horror and action and to ground the exciting or thrilling sequences. Comedies benefit and ground us when they also include serious and deep moments.

It's different when a tone — or tones — are established early and then completely change. One example is the movie, *The Invention of Lying*. It starts out as a fun comedy with an amazing premise and then becomes a serious movie. Our minds and emotions prepare for one thing, so if the piece sets that up then suddenly changes and becomes something else we feel jarred. The audience will feel that their trust has been violated.

I always say, if things are going to get more serious, darker, magical, and so on, that should be hinted at, foreshadowed, or mixed in early, so the audience knows what to expect. As with character arcs, tones can gradually evolve, but should not seem inconsistent or jarring.

Some coverage templates ask if a script's tone is consistent, so Readers need to consider this.

Appropriate to the Subject

We also want the tone to be appropriate to the subject. If it's not then this must be stated early on. We need to know that there will be dark comedic moments in *Dexter* and *The Handmaid's Tale*. An audience will accept tones that go against the subject if this has been established early and remains consistent.

For example, when *The Office* first aired I remember feeling uncomfortable and squirmy and wasn't sure I could keep watching. But I did, and came to love and appreciate the "cringe humor" tone. Other tones that don't adhere to expectations and have succeeded are shows like *What We Do in the Shadows*. Or *Pen15* — which is described as an "American cringe comedy" — that's now a subgenre!

Two period pieces initially shocked me because of their quirky tone, but I then adapted to, appreciated, and enjoyed both for their unexpected bizarre and funny tones: The movie *The Favourite,* and the TV show *The Great,* both by Tony McNamara.

What Does Your Title Say?

What tone would we expect from something called *Cats*? *Euphoria*? *Paris is Burning*? *Big Daddy*? *Moonlight*? Or even *Dexter*?

These days we usually know what something is about before seeing it, but some companies will ask in their coverage templates if the title reflects the piece's genre or tone.

> **American Pie** was originally *East Great Falls High.* The original title seems more specific, but it doesn't quite suggest a comedy.
>
> **Pretty Woman** was *3,000* (after how much was paid for her). The new title may not convey what it was truly about, but it's better than a number that might make one think it was about a bigger army than *300.*
>
> **A Boy's Life** became *E.T.* Probably better, because if memory serves, that title was used for a magazine about camping and fishing.
>
> **The Cut-Whore Killings** became *Unforgiven.* (Yeah, I'm not even going to comment.)
>
> But **Dear White People**? Perfection.

Am I Allowed to Laugh?

The logline and pitch can describe a lot, but it's often the tone and execution that lets us know if we can laugh, cry, be terrified, inspired, moved, provoked, upended and educated, squirm from fear, or cringe-laugh.

I have read titles that I believed would be comedic and realized they weren't, and I had to adjust. For some gatekeepers or execs, that is an automatic point against the project.

To recap: A script should establish its tone right away (even in the title if possible), keep that tone consistent, and add tonal nuances early if they're necessary.

Exercises

1. Find a specific writer, director, writer/director, showrunner (someone who created a TV series), or producer, and see if you can identify a certain tone they often utilize, such as I did with Ryan Murphy. Some good examples are Quentin Tarantino, Spike Lee, Woody Allen (before

and after the 1990's) and Alfred Hitchcock. Those are a bit obvious. Can you name some other recent examples and types of tone they might be known for?

2. There is a fun video on the internet, where someone changed the tone of *Mrs. Doubtfire* from a comedy to a horror film by editing certain clips.

There was a funny meme pretending to be from a *TV Guide* excerpt that read:

> *The Wizard of Oz*: Transported to a surreal landscape, a young girl kills the first person she meets and then teams up with three strangers to kill again.

Choose two to three popular films or TV series and consider how a totally different tone would affect the plot and other story elements. Write an appropriate logline to convey the different tone.

For example, if I look at the logline of the broad comedy, *The Hangover*:

> A Las Vegas-set comedy centered around three groomsmen who lose their about-to-be-wed buddy during their drunken misadventures then must retrace their steps in order to find him.

I could make it into a serious drama by stating:

> Three men wake up from unconsciousness to find their friend has gone missing, and a dangerous, lethal beast locked in the room with them.

3. What tones (and perhaps subject matter) would you expect from the following script titles? And if you know the movie, what tones might one expect if they didn't know it?

A. *Jackass*
B. *The Squid and the Whale*
C. *Brazil*
D. *It Happened One Night*
E. *42*
F. *Precious*
G. *Twelve Monkeys*
H. *Million Dollar Baby*

12

Pacing

What.... Does... That... Even... Mean?

Pace is the forward movement/momentum of a script. It's incredible to watch a movie or read a script that keeps us engulfed, engaged, and entertained, where events and tension escalate, surprises us, and then, when the wonderful ride suddenly stops, we feel exhilarated and satisfied.

Much like tone, pace is something a Reader or audience can feel and often isn't noticed *except when it's not going well.* And much like air, it's integral, sustains what's going on, and also shouldn't be noticed.

Like a good musical composition, a well-paced movie includes breaks and rests, long and short moments, and other changes in rhythm. A script with good pacing doesn't have repetitive beats or overly long scenarios and keeps us invested.

Finally, good pacing isn't just for thrilling, scary, or action-packed scripts which have an expectation of being "fast-paced." With good pacing, the plot of *any type* of film will move forward in a succinct and lean manner, taking us on the ride, no matter how scary, dreamy-romantic, funny, or oddball the script is.

Pacing and Page Count

Remember, with screenplays, one page usually equals one minute of screen time, so we can often tell how a script might do in terms of pacing simply by noting its length.

Most scripts fall between 90 and 120 pages. Family films and comedies are usually expected to be closer to the 90-100 range, and more complicated fare can go longer. Also, some action, thriller, or horror movies may have less dialogue and more quick-moving action, so some of those can also be on the 90- to110-page scale.

Jon Spaihts, Denis Villeneuve, and Eric Roth's *Dune* was 110 pages long. Both Kenneth Branagh's *Belfast* and Rebecca Hall's *Passing* were 95 pages. Tracey Scott Wilson's *Respect* was 105 pages. Charise Castro Smith & Jared Bush's *Encanto* was 100 pages and contained song lyrics within the script.

I often caution writers that when slogging through a pile of scripts, if there's one over 120 pages, a Reader or an executive may assume that script will feel too long. And often we might turn out to be wrong. Lesson: Don't always judge a script by its page count.

The opposite can also be true. When receiving a feature script that's 78-pages long, besides being happy that we'll get the same amount of money for reading less, we might assume that many elements will be underdeveloped or skipped. Or we might expect the pace to be choppy.

I often state the following in coverage notes for lengthy scripts:

> The script is a little long; consider trimming it. Executives get a pile of scripts and sometimes they make an adverse judgment towards ones that are over 120 pages. They might put it on the bottom of their reading pile, or at the very least, assume that the piece will be dense or slow.

How Structure Can Affect Pacing

When a script leaves a Reader with a feeling that the pace is too slow, fast, or clunky, that is often a symptom of structural problems.

Often the pace of a screenplay can feel slow or bogged down when it doesn't have a protagonist who is pursuing a high stakes goal by the end of Act One. Ditto if there's no inciting incident by about page ten. Or if it fails to escalate obstacles and interweave active subplots in Act Two. Things get slow when a script misses the mark of hitting rock bottom at the end of Act Two, or when it lacks an active, protagonist-driven battle in Act Three.

Finally, Act Three should take us on the biggest ride of the whole piece. If all these things, and more, aren't happening then the pace will feel slow.

It will also feel slow if the structure feels episodic and situations or conflicts appear then disappear. If it switches from one situation to another or if a protagonist reacts to, rather than drives events, or if there are too many time jumps, then momentum will feel clunky.

Readers should try to look at the root cause of pacing troubles, so that they can offer suggestions.

For example, rather than writing:

> The pace seems to slow down at the end of Act One.

I might write:

> By the end of Act One, the protagonist still seems to be contemplating, rather than actively pursuing, a high stakes goal. They should drive both events and momentum into Act Two.

Just writing the note, "The pace needs improving," is as effective as a director telling an actor, "More feeling!" It's a vague term that addresses an effect rather than going to the root of the problem to help solve it.

How Character Can Affect Pacing

A character's *investment in their goal* can heighten drama, stakes, tension, and affect the pace. If a protagonist's goal is to get a pencil from a store, that doesn't feel very exciting and it will negatively affect the pace.

Pacing will also suffer if a character wants something big but doesn't get it. For example: May wants to win an art competition but it's a small one and there are 40 bigger ones coming up. Stakes should be high and consequences dire. Getting a pencil from a store will seem more dire if the protagonist must do so in a fascist pencil-less world that kills people who go against the state's "Lead is Dead" philosophy.

Backstory can help with stakes, tension, and pace if it helps us understand why the goal is so big or the obstacles so formidable to a character — even if we don't identify with it. (See the citation in Chapter 6 of "filling a dirt hole in *Parks and Recreation*").

As stated in Chapter 6, Character, if a character doesn't care about the goal, then the audience won't either. And if the audience doesn't care, things will feel slow.

Readers should explain this in the coverage. For example:

> Momentum, pace, tension, and stakes might increase if the audience understood why Luis has to get to Wyoming. Right now, he gets in the car and drives there to see his stepmother, but what are the stakes or consequences? Is there a time limit? What would happen if he failed?

Sometimes several characters will serve the same purpose when one or two might suffice. Imagine how it would affect the pace of *The Empire Strikes Back* if Luke first trained with Yoda, and then went to Boda, then Moda, and then Abe Vigoda (look him up — he was a national treasure, RIP).

How Editing Can Help

Looking for tight dialogue, making sure all scenes forward the plot, and noting repetitive sequences are some ways to judge whether the plot and pace of a script move along swimmingly.

Flashbacks, narration, and voice-overs can help when used sparingly. A note I often give is that flashbacks should inform plot, character, or conflict and should be quick, so that we get back to the main story ASAP. Flashbacks take us backwards, and because of that, they shouldn't be used too often or go on for too long. The same is true for narration and voice-over. Like flashbacks, they should inform and heighten, not distract or stop momentum for too long.

Style and grammar count, too. Mistakes, typos, and errors take us out of the story. Keeping the writing tight, active, and as lean as it can be will help the pacing.

Keep an eye out for passive voice. There's a sluggishness that comes from stage directions with terms like *is walking* and *are going*.

Feel the difference between these two lines:

> Geraldo is walking to the store.

> Geraldo walks to the store.

Make certain that active verbs are used and generic terms like "walk" are avoided. Used different verbs so we can see *how* the character walks, because that can inject energy (which helps pace) and inform character:

> Geraldo frolicked to the store.

> Geraldo bolted to the store.

It's even okay if a script includes a few relevant details:

> Geraldo bolted to the store, a bomb ticking in his hand.

> Geraldo frolicked to the new time-traveler's store.

Look for words that could be cut, like *begin* or *start*:

> Tasha began to eat her sandwich.

> Tasha ate her sandwich.

These are small and sometimes subliminal details that can bog down and slow the action. Changes like these also add more white space on the page, which makes for a better read.

Keep an eye out for long passes that can be broken up into smaller chunks, separated by white space. For example:

> Leofric ran to the curtains of the castle, ripped them off, tied them around his waist, and swung from the ceiling, sword in hand, leaping to the chandelier and gripping it. From this precarious position, he saw his prey down below, the nefarious Middlemuster Trio, twirling their greasy moustaches as they chuckled over their precious treasure, the Lady Swantenfein.

That's a lot to take in and should be broken up:

> Leofric ran to the curtains of the castle, ripped them off, and tied them around his waist.

> He swung from the ceiling, sword in hand, leaping to the chandelier and gripped it.

> From this precarious position, he saw his prey down below, the nefarious Middlemuster Trio!

Adding space between lines and breaking up long paragraphs helps to frame important points, keep things short, and keep things moving. I often write the following note:

> Break up long paragraphs and descriptions. Executives and readers like white space. It keeps things moving and makes sure that various elements are framed and don't get lost.

All that said, shorter isn't always better if it results in a script that is bland, sluggish, or vague.

> Moshe saw the guy and they fought a tad.

Compare to:

> Battle worn, scarred, and dying, Moshe, with his
> final breaths, assailed the mountainous Philistinian
> regiment, one dying man against a Titanian army,
> mowing down multitudes and hacking at limbs….

Enter Late, Leave Early

A well-known mantra in the screenplay world is to enter a scene late and leave early. Pace can really move when we arrive in the middle of action or a conversation (but can still understand what's going on) and leave at a high point. This is different than theatrical plays, because films are a more visual and quicker medium that can span many more locations.

It's lovely to have a scene in the coroner's office with a dame (always a dame) looking under a sheet and exclaiming, "That's not my husband's body."

We don't need:

> Dame: That's not my husband's body!
>
> Coroner: Are you sure?
>
> Dame: Of course, I'm sure. We've been married for
> 14 years. Let me tell you how we met. You see, I
> was born in a small house in Georgia. The year was
> 19-ought 35…

When we see beats being repeated, or precious dialogue and moments taking too long, then it's time to make some notes about pacing.

Is This Even Needed?

Writers often say they need to "kill their darlings." A writer may love a character, scene, subplot, or line even though it doesn't serve the plot and halts momentum. I often write:

> If a scene can be cut without affecting the plot, then
> consider heightening stakes or conflict, deepening
> or informing character, or perhaps cutting or
> combining it with another one.

This can be painful for a writer to hear, but all elements must further the plot. In fact, on one coverage template I was given, that was one of the questions we had to assess and score: "Does each scene further the plot?"

The best scenes make us laugh, fall in love, give information, and inform characters, all while forwarding the plot.

Too Many Devices Spoil the Broth

Certain devices can add innovation, information, and originality as well as help pace and tone. Some voice-overs add more flavor or let us inside a character's mind. A flashback can make a goal, stakes, or conflict richer. Dream and fantasy sequences can add color, layers, or humor.

However, I often read scripts with too many devices. If a script wants to take us on a roller coaster ride, then we don't want too many slow-downs, distractions, time outs, or indulgences.

A script with five flashbacks, 18 voice-overs, two dream sequences, and 95 camera angles all before the end of Act One? I'm pulled out, yanked, and my roller coaster keeps stopping and starting till I shout "Let me off" because it isn't a ride. It's a limp. It may be infuriating to hear me repeat that it's all an art, and not an exact science, but it is.

Exercises

Chop it up! Turn these verbose and dense chunks of information into lines that are more active, engaging and that keep momentum going. Use active verbs and cut lines that are not needed:

1, Billy and Jocelyn sat in the tree house and thought about a twig they saw when their older brother, Roger, and his four friends started climbing up the ladder to join them. Roger and his friends climbed up the ladder rung. First the one on the bottom and then the next one. They then went to the third. And then the fourth. It was a nice day. The sun was out. Roger said a hilarious line about leaves. It was hilarious. They then went up the next rung… Oh and it was also tense…

2. Leandra pulled out her sword and raised it. She gripped it tighter and walked over to her opponent, Gregor. Gregor also walked over to her. He also had a sword. The two faced each other and circled around. They studied and eyed each other, and Leandra waved her sword around a lot more. Gregor looked imposing. Leandra said, "You are mean." Gregor answered, "That is true. But it is because my parents were ogre people and they liked eating berries, so, ya know." Leandra stopped, thought about that, and went, "Huh." It affected her. She thought back to 1342 when she bathed in the big river. It was a wet river, yes indeedydoo…

3. Doug: Let's drive to Calcutta.

    Chris: Dude, you can't drive to Calcutta.

Doug: Well, not with that negative attitude.

Chris: No, I mean there's water and stuff.

Doug: Why do you have to stomp on my dreams?

Chris: It's your dream to drive to Calcutta?

Doug: Well, I want to go.

Chris: Well, we can fly there. Why do you want to go?

Doug: Dunno. Thought it would be cool.

The two then decided they should figure out how to get tickets and go. (End of Act One.)

13

Craft and Presentation

Fancy Words for Grammar and Formatting

For film and TV writing, mechanics break down into two categories: formatting and grammar. Formatting means using the screenplay conventions specific to the type of project: feature films, single-camera series, and multi-camera television all have slightly different formatting rules. Grammar is exactly what we think but there are some specifics that a script must follow.

This category in a coverage template may be called *presentation*, which refers to the mechanics, or *craft*, which also means mechanics (although it sounds like it should refer to the creativity).

Grammar and formatting affect the read. A script that has this on the first page:

```
INT. SUPERMERKET — DAY

ROGER, 65, and BERTHA, stab each other in
front of the gercrie secshun.
```

...is one that will cause us to stumble over the writing. In the middle of a lovely stabbing scene, the Reader must stop to figure out what the writer meant.

Formatting

There are rules about formatting that need to be obeyed. Some change based on different script formats (half-hour sitcom, feature film, etc.), while others have evolved over time. Still others are set in stone, such as: margins, how to begin and end a script (FADE IN, FADE OUT, and THE END), what is capitalized and what isn't, and so on.

Many writers couldn't state the proper font or margin specifics because most screenwriting apps handle these things automatically. As a Reader it's important to learn the format-specific rules that apply to a script. Not only can incorrect formatting distract and detract from the story, but many buyers and agents will assume that the writer is not a professional and won't give the script a chance.

Resources for Learning More About Script Formatting

Learn formatting from such lovely books as:

* *The New Elements of Standard Screenplay Format* by Jean-Paul Ouelette

* *The Hollywood Standard: The Complete and Authoritative Guide to Script Format and Style* by Christopher Riley

Use lovely software such as:

* *Final Draft* Offers a free 30-day trial.

* *Celtx* Has a basic subscription-based plan.

* Movie Magic *Screenwriter*

And read lovely examples of scripts on such sites as:

* *Script Slug* (scriptslug.com)

* *IMSDB* aka, the *Internet Movie Screenplay Database* (imsdb.com)

* *Drew's Script-o-Rama* (script-o-rama.com)

* *Simply Scripts* (simplyscripts.com)

This isn't a full list, and I don't get a commission on any of these.

Grammatical Errors

Software can help with spelling but it won't catch everything, especially in creative works. For example, a spelling checker won't recognize film industry jargon like *slugline*. Or some lovely non-traditional character names, like *JJIGTFDTTTTT*.

Also, normal grammar rules don't apply if we have characters speaking in dialect or slang. A character speaking slang adds taste and flavor to a script, but it shouldn't be so overdone that it makes for a difficult read.

Consider this exchange from the movie, *Straight Outta Compton*:

```
                    EAZY
          Now where the money at?

                    TONE
          Man, you heard what happen? My best
          runner got cracked...
```

We know this is slang and we know why it's being used. Never make a Reader wonder if it's intentional or not.

What Readers Should Do and What They Don't Have to Do

Readers: *Do not* cite or correct loads and loads of grammar and formatting mistakes, especially in shorter coverage. That is the job of an editor or proofreader, not us.

What I often do is state that there are one or two typos or errors, and perhaps give an example.

> There are a couple of typos and grammatical errors here and there such as writing "it's mother" rather than "its mother" on page 9, or how it says CLARRY on page 41.

I do this because once I stated that there were typos in a coverage and the writer didn't believe me, so now I give examples.

If there is an overall formatting error, I might state that.

For example:

> The page numbers should be in the upper right-hand corner, not the bottom.

> Give ages for all characters when they are first introduced. It makes a difference if people are in their 20s vs. 40s, etc.
>
> If you have parentheses within dialogue and there's no dialogue below it, just make it an action line.

I cite these because they are rules that the writer can learn, address, and fix themselves. This would usually be done for coverage that writers receive, not executives.

If I'm writing coverage for an agent or a company, I don't need to bother them with specifics of grammar and formatting mistakes. I can simply tell them that there are quite a few typos or formatting errors. Like Readers, executives may be judged harshly for passing something up the line to their bosses that seems unprofessional.

Readers need to check the heck out of their own grammar when doing coverage. And I don't just mean knowing basic grammar rules. For example, elements such as character names must be spelled correctly.

Reasons for Errors

Readers must report mistakes but hold off on judgements. The writer might be dyslexic, have spelling or grammar issues, or English might not be their first language.

I worked with a new writer who had dyslexia, and we focused a lot on the script's structure and story. I saw many mistakes but that was not what I was hired to advise on. They came to writing at a later age and didn't have many writer friends, so I asked if they knew someone who was a teacher or a great proofreader, to help them out. I told the that people who aren't in the industry may think it's thrilling to be part of *the movie biz* and gladly take a look-see. They got a friend who teaches English to proofread, and the friend was glad to help because it was a movie script!

Exercises

1. In the following example, first see how it feels to read this opening for a script. Imagine you are the agent who received it. Now, correct both the formatting and grammar as best as possible. What do you feel are the biggest issues? What might not bother you as much?

```
INT. A HOUSE IN A FORST AND ITS COLD.
ALSO IT'S 1899.

RACHEL is a girl. And of age. She thinks
a lot about things. She's thinking about
```

her mother's cooking. Right now she gets
would for a fire.

>   RACHEL (is sad)
>   Mom. I'm getting would. Poor mom is
>   sick. I hope she feels better.

An Scottish comes along and speaks gaelic
in his mind.

>   SCOTTISH
>   Dia dhuit!

2. Compare the scene above, and how it feels, to the following examples where the stage directions utilize "proper grammar" but the dialogue doesn't (and shouldn't). What does the use of dialect or slang, evoke?

This is an excerpt from the feature film, *Belfast*. These are kids playing on the streets of Belfast, Ireland in 1969:

EXT. BACK ENTRY DAY

MOIRA appears at the top of the entry.

>   MOIRA
>   Hey Buddy!

A boy slowly turns. He carries a
primitive home-made wooden sword held
aloft in one hand, and in the other an
upturned dustbin lid, that he holds
before him, like a shield.

This is BUDDY.

>   MOIRA (CONT'D)
>   Your Ma's callin' you. Yer tea's
>   ready.

BUDDY rejoices.

>   MOIRA (CONT'D)
>   All the rest of you too.

He runs to the top of the entry.

And this is an excerpt from the feature film, *King Richard*. It takes place in 1989, and Serena and Venus Williams' father, Richard, is from the city of Compton. He's talking to a tennis pro in Beverly Hills.

Richard stands in the pro shop in his
TENNIS ATTIRE, when a TENNIS PRO arrives
with a SHOPPING BAG.

                    TENNIS PRO
          Grounds crew threw out most of 'em.
          Got a few here but they look pretty
          dead.

                    RICHARD
          They not dead to us.

          Richard looks in the bag. It's filled with
          RATTY OLD TENNIS BALLS. Richard takes it
          thankfully and without shame, heading out
          with his bounty as we hear —

                    RICHARD (V.O.)
          Where I grew up, in Louisiana,
          Seedy Grove. Tennis was not a game
          peoples played. We was too busy
          running from the Klan. But here it
          is...

This is an excerpt from the TV show *Ozark*. In it, a married couple from
the city, Wendy and Marty, argue with a self-described hillbilly (she will
not be called a redneck) named Darlene:

                    DARLENE
          How many times you think I'm gone
          let you disrespect me and get away
          with it.

                    WENDY
          You don't understand. It's us who
          require your respect, or more
          specifically the cartel. You cannot
          out-gun them, you cannot out-run
          them--

                    MARTY
          We just need to know what's going
          on. Today your armed militia
          completely stopped construction on
          the casino. And we -- we can't have
          that. This casino is moving forward
          and I thought we had an
          understanding.

          DARLENE moves closer to MARTY. WENDY eyes
          DARLENE suspiciously.

                    DARLENE
          Ain't no understanding. I lost my
          Jacob after you and this goddamn
          casino.

          Her eyes cross to WENDY.

```
                    DARLENE (CONT'D)
          Your... maiden burned my crops for
          this damn casino.
```

3. Come up with three different types of characters or situations where incorrect grammar, as in slang, could be used.

14

Marketability

Big Bucks!!!! Or Baby Bucks?

Show biz is a biz.

When companies look at coverage of a script they want to know if they can market and make money off it, so Readers must state their opinions and assessment of a script's marketability. This wasn't an easy question for me when I was starting out. I knew that *Avengers 22 Electric Boogaloo* would have a big budget, but what about that darling little independent film about a brother and a sister competing in a Monopoly tournament in Boise, Idaho? We all have some sort of sense about how expensive and/or lucrative a project may be but a professional Reader must consider many aspects.

❓ But What about Art?

For all the filmmakers who will say, "I got into this industry to make art, not commerce" — don't despair. People will always want a good story, an amazing world, or an escape. Sometimes they want to learn or become inspired. Sometimes they want to keep up with the latest and greatest, check out what all the buzz is about, and possibly see a star or two. Try to think of marketability as a tool that helps one make their art and not as an adversary. Until a person's name, brand, or franchise can sell on its own, marketing is necessary to sell a story.

Budget

In the beginning… was the word. Or a few of them. And some flipbooks or silent films. In order to make money, the box office *take* (how much it earns) must be much larger than the budget (how much it costs to make). Both budget and box office numbers have risen astronomically over the years.

The first feature length film (meaning it was six reels at 18 minutes a reel) was Cecil B. DeMille's 1914 *The Squaw Man*. It was a great success for the Jesse L. Lasky Feature Play Company thanks to the company's general manager, Samuel Goldfish (later Goldwyn). It cost about $45,000 to produce and earned about $250,000.

James Cameron's 2009 film, *Avatar*, cost about $237 million to make and ended up earning about $280 billion.

While it might be obvious to tell if a script will require a big or small budget, it takes thoughtful analysis to determine if the script's budget is a liability.

Bigger Is Better?

We always hear that in order to make money we have to spend it — but it. has to be spent right. *Avengers: Endgame* had many things going for it: the Marvel brand and the *Avengers* name, as well as the name/brand of all the individual superheroes that had their own movies and/or had appeared in earlier *Avengers* movies. On top of that, it was a "going out of business" sale. People like me who had stopped watching the other Marvel movies thought, "Hmm, if this is the last one, then I'll see it. Oh, but first I must go back and watch all the previous ones for context."

Big budget movies can be marketable when they already have a brand, a following, stars or a big director attached, or a built-in audience. But not always. One of the biggest cautionary tales in Hollywood is Michael Cimino's flop, *Heaven's Gate,* which he made in 1980 after his Oscar-winning success with *The Deer Hunter* in 1978. The film's $44 million budget (about $117 million in today's dollars) and poor performance at the box office ($3.5 million gross in the United States) ended up causing bad publicity, an issue with the production company, and along with some other box office disappointments, a curtailing on the lavish budgets given to 1970's directors going forward. It also ultimately led to the shuttering of United Artists, the oldest surviving movie studio at the time.

Low Budgets, Big Successes

While studios may buy some low-budget or independent films to serve as Oscar bait, make a star happy, or tell a good story, even micro-budgeted projects have a chance to hit the zeitgeist, strike a nerve, and go on to do very well. *The Blair Witch Project* had a budget of $100,000 and made over $248 million. *Little Miss Sunshine* cost $8 million and made $101 million. And in 1976, *Rocky* was made for $1 million, earned over $200 million, won three Oscars, launched the career of Sylvester Stallone, and spawned many sequels and reboots, including three *Creed* movies starring Michael B. Jordan that were helmed, produced and/or written by Ryan Coogler.

Giving Notes on Budget

So, while budget can be a factor in a script's ability to make money, we can't always say that a budget of a particular size is necessarily good or bad. That means the writer, Reader, agent, execs, and marketing teams must weigh how big or small the budget is against how much money it could make.

For example, if a coverage template has a category called *marketability*, Readers could consider some of the following:

- Does the script have any famous or really successful actors, directors, or writers already attached (committed to doing it)?
- Does the script have roles that could attract big talent? This means characters who are active, complex, have wonderful arcs, and are inspiring.
- Is the script based on a known entity such as a successful book, franchise, a prequel, sequel, or remake?
- Is it a type of project that has been successful in the past or currently? For example, as *Jurassic Park* films do well, can we think of another type of huge adventure — perhaps where characters actually go back in time and fight actual dinosaurs?
- Can it do well in the global market? Will it spawn sequels or a series?
- Maybe it hits the zeitgeist, such as both the 2019 film, *Bombshell* (a group of women take on Fox News head Roger Ailes and the toxic atmosphere he presided over at the network) and the 2019 Apple TV series, *The Morning Show*, based on Brian Stelter's book *Top of the Morning: Inside the Cutthroat World of Morning TV*. Both examined the sexist world of news organizations during the #MeToo movement.
- Is the script based on a person, time, or event that people are interested in, such as *The Crown*?

- Can it sell adorable Baby Yoda toys? (Merchandising.)

When assessing the marketability of a script, look for anything that will hit the current mood, attract large audiences, and make more money than it costs to produce.

Here is an example of something I wrote in the *marketability* section of a script coverage:

> In a time where Hollywood looks for unique and diverse stories and points of view, this one hits on quite a few. Not only does it depict various ethnicities and cultures, but it also goes right to the heart of homeless people and their stories. The locations and images will be incredible, and the messages will be very moving and eye-opening. Go further with some clarity and structure — especially activating the story — as that will help attract A-list talent, which can always make a film even more marketable.

Who Is the Audience?

One question that Readers must often answer is, "What platforms might this project be right for?" This used to be a question specifically for TV projects but the lines are now blurred between what were once distinct channels of distribution: feature films, broadcast television, cable, and streaming content. Today the concern is less about the type of distributor and more about the brand.

For example, two female detectives solving crimes using the latest technology may fit on one network well, but if we add vampires and make the women 19 years old, that network may lose interest. I wrote a pilot that had an ensemble cast and finding the right buyer or platform depended on who got more screen time — the 50-something character or the 17-year-old — even though the script told both stories.

The truth is, most distribution platforms try to hit a certain demographic or niche, which is how those platforms define their brand.

Finding the Niche for Networks

To know where a project might find a home, there are often announcements of what different platforms are looking for or buying (subscribe to *Deadline*). In the beginning, HBO was "not TV" — meaning it was the place to go for edgy shows where men were in prison or Mafia guys gushed over ducks in their pool. Showtime experimented with gay and Latin fare, and AMC and FX each had their own approaches and feel. There are networks that appeal to younger people, networks that want soapy dramas or the biggest reality shows, and so on.

Over time, platforms can change. Before CBS took on the *Survivor* and *CSI* franchises, a network executive described its audience as being "65 to death," with its biggest shows being *Diagnosis Murder* or *Murder She Wrote*. This is the same network that, in 1970, threw out its successful series about people never getting off an island (*Gilligan's Island*) or rich people moving to the country and loving pigs (*Green Acres*) to make a huge cultural shift. They introduced three ground-breaking and innovative shows about a bigot, a single woman making it on her own, and a show that stated that war was not fun. (And the shows were... *All in the Family, The Mary Tyler Moore Show*, and *M*A*S*H*, respectively.)

What about Streaming?

And then there's streaming, which changed the landscape of what we watch, when we watch it, and how often. It changed how many episodes a series may have in a season. (Although cable had already halved the broadcast orders from around 22 to 13, 10, 8, etc.) It also changed how many seasons they ran. BBC shows could be six a year and run for the life cycle of human history (*Dr. Who*), or just 2-3 seasons (Ricky Gervais' *The Office*). But then along came Netflix, Hulu, Amazon Prime, Apple, HBO Max, and a gajillion more. The good news was: Oooh! So many markets needing content! The bad news was that many wanted projects that already had big names attached, and weren't willing to run them for very long.

So, while it seems like anything could be on Netflix — *Big Mouth, Tiger King,* and *Bridgerton* — different departments inside Netflix claim to have their own specifics mandates. Similarly, Hulu and Amazon both state they're looking for different types of projects at different moments.

As Readers, we need to stay up-to-date.

More is More for Movies?

Another factor in assessing marketability for feature films is looking at who the audience for a script might be. Built-in audiences are always attractive. For example, it was a no-brainer making the *Harry Potter* movies given the size of the books' fanbase. The same goes for *The Hunger Games*, Marvel movies, many sequels, reboots, remakes, prequels, and origin stories. Stars also bring their own audiences. Look at the (third) remake of *A Star Is Born*. The film already had name recognition and the two stars did as well.

Executives always want to hit the *four quadrants* if possible: Males over 25, Males under 25, Females over 25, and Females under 25 (the ages may shift a bit). Some examples of ones that successfully did so were *Star Wars,*

The Hunger Games, and *Jurassic Park.* And while all movies can't be all things to all people, hitting all four quadrants ensures that the audience will be large enough to earn a profit even when the cost of production is huge.

Giving Notes on Potential Audience

Companies look to coverage to find out if there is an audience for a script, as well as who the audience is. It's often useful to list projects that have similar audiences to the one we're giving notes on: *Dear White People*, *Selena*, and *Euphoria* have their audiences, and *Chicago Hope* has theirs.

When assessing marketability, Readers need to suggest whether or not a script would be a good fit for a specific distribution platform. So it's important to know the various platforms, their audiences, and what might appeal to them. Sometimes we're asked if a TV script fits with a certain network or platform. And of course, if we're reading for a specific company like HBO or Disney, we should state if it fits their particular brand.

Is Everyone Looking for the Same Things?

Even though most companies want to make money, want a built-in audience, brand or name recognition, a good story, or meaty role for a star, not everyone assesses a project the same way. A-list actors look for compelling roles, or sometimes, a big paycheck or franchise.

Actors and Agents

Agents that represent A-list actors and directors want to please their clients, give them meaty scripts, and they hope for a big payday in return. Agents and managers looking for scripts to sell or to rep the writers want to know if the script is lucrative or has a market, and if they can make money off this writer and their work for a long time. That's why they ask, "What else you got?" They want to make sure that a prospective writing client is not a one-hit wonder. Although some agents are fine with selling one specific script, and getting their clients more assignments, many nag them to write their next one.

Producers

Although different companies look for different things, they all want to make money. A broadcast network wants a show that could run for at least 6-7 seasons since the big money comes from *syndication* (being shown later as reruns on different stations that have paid to show them).

It costs a lot of money to make popular broadcast TV shows — think of the actors on *Friend*s — in the last two seasons each lead was paid $1 million per episode. Once a show has made about 100 episodes, those can then be syndicated to other networks or platforms. Streaming and subscription platforms want prominent shows to keep the money flowing, the buzz buzzing, the subscribers subscribing, and the eyeballs... eyeballing?

While they all want to make money, many also want more: agents and execs want to make a name for themselves, and most want projects that can spawn sequels, seasons, or subscribers.

Screenplay Competitions

Competitions are a bit different — yet similar. While coverage for a contest will also have a category asking about marketability, the people who read this coverage are often not sellers or buyers but they are *promoters*. Make no mistake, quite a few competitions want to say they discovered the next big thing, and I've been in the room for deliberations when that phrase has been uttered. But overall, many respected competitions are trying to herald good works and good writing, and quite a few want to champion independent films. The Nicholl Fellowship often rewards excellent writing, as does the Slamdance Screenplay Competition, which was created in response to other competitions that increasingly rewarded potential commercial and studio successes over all other types of projects. So, while the writing is the main part of how competition scripts are judged, Readers will also often be asked how marketable a script is.

Timely

Hollywood has changed a lot these past few years alone. A liberal pundit recently said that the *Friends* reunion show must have shocked younger viewers. A show about six straight white people? That wouldn't fly anymore — and it shouldn't. I gently warn writers that Hollywood has become more sensitive, so a few things don't fly anymore, and that a project might be marketable if it has female, Black, trans, gay, Latinx, or Asian leads and issues. *Black Panther, Captain Marvel, Shang-Chi and the Legend of the Ten Rings*, and *Wonder Woman* succeeded, and other superheroes can now be gay and trans, Muslim, and AAPI. Diversity is marketable. It's not just good business. It's good and right. It's also an example of how timeliness can impact marketability.

There are many projects that can address timely issues in subversive ways. Shadi Petosky, the transgender showrunner of a children's show that was called *Danger & Eggs*, had a masterful episode where the characters talked about how there wasn't just one way to be an adult, and people can like or not like broccoli if they want. Petoski addressed larger issues of conformity by making the story about vegetables. Period pieces often depict racism and homophobic issues, and those conflicts are heightened because of the times. And sometimes just casting diverse people in a period piece like *The Great* or *Bridgerton* can go a long way.

A script can be marketable because it makes a statement about important timely issues — no matter how or when it does so.

Great Script but Who Will Pay to See the Movie?

When I was a development executive at a low-budget company, I remembered a friend's amazing and very well written low-budget script. In it, two young brothers were abandoned by their mother, and one had to prostitute himself to protect his younger sibling. It was well-written, but my boss said, "Yes, it's a great script, but no one will pay to see this movie." This was a wake-up call for me. The writing, story, and characters may all be there, but would people want to pay to spend time in such a harsh environment? Maybe. During Covid I had a hard time getting back to watching *The Handmaid's Tale*. Meanwhile *Schitt's Creek* and *Ted Lasso* did very well because people needed a happy, light, and sweet escape.

In summary: When reading a script, we need to have an eye on how easy it might be to market, how profitable it may be, if it will attract names, has a built-in audience or brand, addresses current and timely issues, and will put tushies in seats.

Exercises

1. Target audiences: What kind of audiences might see the following films and why? Think of ages, demographics, fans, class, interest, etc. Who might not?

   A. Hulu's *Only Murders in the Building* starring Steve Martin, Martin Short, and Selena Gomez. Logline: Three strangers who share an obsession with true crime suddenly find themselves caught up in one? Listed as Comedy, Crime, Drama.

   B. Freeform's *Grown-ish*: A spin-off of ABC's *Black-ish*, the oldest daughter is off to college and must live outside the nest, dealing with drugs, sex, and relationships along the way. Listed as Comedy, Drama.

   C. The 2021 feature, *Dune*. A noble family becomes embroiled in a war for control over the galaxy's most valuable asset while its heir becomes troubled by visions of a dark future. Listed as Action, Adventure, Drama.

2. Research the following: (Do a Google search for *budgets*, *box office*, etc.)

A. What is a very expensive movie — the budget was over $100 million — that was very profitable? (Such as the example earlier in this chapter, *Avatar*.)

B. What was considered a low-budget movie (less than $2 million) that made a huge profit? (So, the gap between budget and box office was huge.)

C. What was a big-budget movie (over $100 million) that was considered unsuccessful or a "flop" (made less than half of that)?

3. For the following three fictional projects, state if they are marketable or not and explain why or why not. And if they don't seem to be, is there anything that might help?

A. Feature, comedy film: Four male friends decide to open four pop-up businesses in four days to pay for one guy's wedding.

B. Feature, science fiction film: In a post-apocalyptic world following a huge nuclear war, humans and animals fused and then spawned new generations of interspecies creatures, all warring for dominance.

C. Feature, historical drama film: In 8000 BC Egypt, bread was invented.

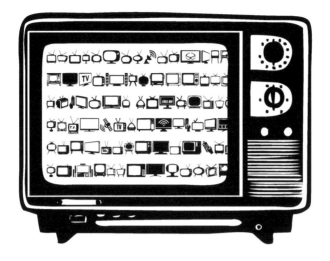

15

TV

Where It's Okay to Act Out

TV Story Structure

Readers need to know how TV differs from feature films. While feature films generally conform to a three-act structure, TV shows vary wildly, and it would be impossible to go into every type of story structure for television here. That said, most TV series are made up of either one-hour or half-hour episodes and these time limitations have an effect on the story structure.

One-hour shows are traditionally dramas and shot with a single camera (similar to feature films). Half-hour shows are traditionally comedies and are either shot with a single camera or with multiple cameras on a stage in front of a live audience. However, as the TV landscape changes some of these rules can be bent, such as the half-hour drama, one-hour comedy, or the blended genre — the dramedy.

One-Hour Shows

One-hour shows can be standalone, procedural, or serialized. For example, consider *Black Mirror*, *CSI ANYWHERE*, and *Ozark,* respectively. The first is a "one and done," (aka *anthology series*), the second usually has a case, disease, or crime of the week (known as a *procedural)* and the third tells a story over the run of the series (a *long arc*). There are also *limited series* that might last for one or a few seasons, with some elements changing from one season to another. For example, *Fargo* followed a different story each season but with similar themes, *The Crown* and *Bridgerton* jump over years and change cast members, while *Halston* had five episodes and was done.

Different platforms also vary in the different numbers of episodes they order per season. Broadcast network shows (for both half-hour and hour) usually run around 22 episodes per season, while streaming and cable show often have 6-13 episodes. Broadcast makes their big money from a show getting into syndication while cable and streaming usually don't. So, some platforms look for shows that will span many seasons and get watched for years (like *Friends*, *Law & Order*, or *The Simpsons*), while streaming and cable platforms get their money from subscriptions.

Overall, most hour-long shows are similar in formatting to feature films, with act breaks if there are commercials, and usually consist of 5-8 acts.

Here's an example from a groundbreaking show that not enough people watched, called *OZ* (HBO, prison drama):

```
INT. CU ON AUGUSTUS HILL

                HILL
        "Survival of the fittest." One
        hundred and fifty years ago, some
        balding old English guy said that.
        It means      -- the strong survive,
        and the weak can eat shit.


INT. ENTRANCE TO OZ PENETENTIARY -
MORNING

TIM MCMANNUS enters the facility wearing
his usual leather jacket with his bag
slung over his shoulder. As he walks
through the main doors he pauses before a
guard stationed there, looking at him with
an eyebrow raised.

                HILL (V.O.)
        Funny coming from an old guy who
        probably couldn't throw a punch if
        his life depended on it, isn't it?
```

```
MCMANNUS continues past the first guard,
only to find more guards at a makeshift
security station, along with a metal
detector. He makes to walk past the
guards, but they stop him. Even as
MCMANNUS holds up his ID card, the guards
shake their head.

                HILL (V.O.)
        But then again, strength isn't just
        about who's got more muscle these
        days.

MCMANNUS, looking disbelieving,
surrenders his bag and jacket to the
guards, then walks back to go through the
metal detector.
```

See? It looks just like a regular feature film format. This is how it is for most one-hour shows since they are shot with a single camera, which is also known as *film-style* shooting.

Page length will usually indicate whether it's a one-hour or half-hour show. *However*, newer platforms can blur the lines. For broadcast and cable, half-hour shows are approximately 26-40 pages (which I'll get into next), whereas one-hour shows are usually about 50-60 pages long (remember the "one page equals a minute" guideline plus commercial breaks). But streaming platforms are different since they don't schedule shows, and don't have to end on the exact hour or half hour. For all these reasons, we're now seeing some scripts that run for 42 pages, 31, 75, etc.

Half-Hour Shows

Half-hour shows are usually comedies and as stated, can be shot with a single camera, (called *single-cam*) such as *Sex and the City* or *The Office*, or with multiple cameras (*multi-cam*) in front of a live audience, such as *The Big Bang Theory* and *Mom* (many Chuck Lorre shows).

Half-hour comedies are huge on major broadcast networks (ABC, NBC, CBS, and FOX), and where we'll usually find more multi-cam shows. Broadcast comedies, whether single-cam or multi-cam have act breaks that leave room for commercials. They also often have prologues and epilogues.

Act Breaks

Back in the olden days, every TV show had act breaks that were filled with commercials. Today, many cable networks and streaming platforms don't, but for all that do, those *act out* moments — meaning the end of the act — must be strong. Many coverage templates even ask:

> Does it have a strong 3-5 (whatever is appropriate)
> act structure, and does each act (and scene) end on
> a strong moment?

The reasoning is that we don't want to go to commercial and lose our audience. We want to end the teaser, scene, act, and episode on a plot twist, big emotional reaction, or funny joke — even more so than film acts (which are implied in the screenplay but not labeled). Like a film, we want the protagonist to drive events and momentum, but unlike films, we also want audiences to *need to see* what happens next. So, for example, ending a sitcom act with someone saying, "I'm pregnant" and seeing another character's huge reaction would leave the audience wanting to see what happens after the bathroom or snack break.

As more and more platforms do away with commercials (and act and scene delineations), some may not require a script to actually label the act breaks, but we should still feel like they're there. We still want twists and turns, escalations, and momentum, to keep the audience hooked and the plot escalating.

Cold Opens, Teasers, and Tags

Both multi-camera and single-camera shows can have a *cold open* or a *teaser*, and possibly a *tag*. The first two are short scenes found at the start of an episode and the tag is a quick scene at the end. The openers should hook the audience's attention. They can be a funny bit that doesn't relate to the rest of the plot, or a scene or sequence that gets us into the theme of the episode. Usually, the *cold open* leads into the plot and a *teaser* is just a funny bit. The *tag* should be thought of as a cherry on top or "pinning a tail on the donkey," in that the story is resolved, we come back from commercial, and it's a fun extra scene. If it were cut, the story would still be intact and resolved, like an epilogue. (And in syndicated reruns, the tag is often cut to allow time for more commercials.)

Teleplay Formatting

Let's further examine the different categories for how a show is shot: multi-camera (or many cameras) and single-camera because each has their own set of rules for script formatting.

Multi-Camera Scripts

As far as teleplay formatting goes, multi-camera sitcom scripts are completely different from feature film scripts. They usually have 3-5 acts, each act is broken into scenes, and every scene gets a letter. (Ex: Act One Scene A). Also, every act and/or scene starts on a new page.

Often, sluglines are underlined, and the cast that appears in the scene is listed underneath in parentheses. It's also common to number each new day or night as the script progresses, so that by the end we know how many days are depicted. This makes it easy to assess the number of costume, set, lighting, and other changes.

Stage directions are capitalized. Character names are also capitalized in the body of the script when they are first introduced. When they first enter a scene, their name is underlined. The way that dialogue and parentheticals work is also different from films and single-camera shows. If there are stage directions (emotional or physical) attached to a line of dialogue, those are included within that line of dialogue in parentheses and all-caps. (Rather than on their own line like in a feature script.) Stage directions outside of dialogue (regular action) are also capitalized. Oh, and there are bigger spaces between lines of dialogue.

Here's an example from *The Big Bang Theory*:

```
FADE IN:

INT. FERTILITY CLINIC WAITING ROOM - DAY
(DAY 1)

(Leonard, Sheldon, Althea, Extras)

WE OPEN ON LEONARD, A POST DOCTORAL
THEORETICAL PHYSICIST, AN ACTUAL GENIUS -
- HIS IQ IS OFF THE CHARTS. HE SITS
IMPATIENTLY FOR A BEAT, SEES A RUBIK'S
CUBE ON THE TABLE, PICKS IT UP AND SOLVES
IT IN A FEW DEFT MOVES. HIS FRIEND AND
ROOMMATE, SHELDON, ALSO A VERIFIABLE
GENIUS WITH SIMILAR CREDENTIALS, EMERGES
THROUGH A DOOR.

                LEONARD
        Took you long enough.

                SHELDON
        If you had any inkling of what I've
        just been through I think you'd be
        a little more sympathetic.

                LEONARD
        What could you have been through?
        You went in there to make a sperm
        deposit.
```

>   SHELDON
>   Leonard, think about it. We're
>   selling our sperm to a high IQ sperm
>   bank, but we can't guarantee high
>   IQ offspring. Extreme intelligence
>   is as much of a mutation as the
>   migrating eye of a flounder.

Notice in the above example, the slugline is underlined, the day number is listed, the characters in the scene are listed, the stage directions are in capitals, and characters' names are underlined when they enter the scene.

Next, is an example from *Friends*, for a better look at act and scene sluglines, as well as parenthetical stage directions within dialogue:

ACT ONE

SCENE B

FADE IN:

INT. THEATER - FOUR HOURS LATER

(Rachel, Monica, Phoebe, Joey, Chandler, Ross, Aurora)

WE PAN ACROSS EACH OF THE GROUP'S STUNNED FACES AS THE CAST TAKES ITS CURTAIN CALL. THEY ALL WEAR PERIOD COSTIUMES, SOME ARE IN STRAITJACKETS. OUR GROUP OF FRIENDS LEADS A TENTATIVE APPLAUSE. THE CURTAIN CLOSES.

>   PHOEBE
>   Wow.

>   RACHEL
>   I feel violated.

>   MONICA
>   Was I the only one who wanted to
>   peel the skin off my body just to
>   have something else to do?

>   CHANDLER
>   (WHISPERS) Ross. Ten o'clock.

>   ROSS
>   (LOOKS AT HIS WATCH) Is it?

Notice how this example starts with the act number and scene letter at the top, then lists the castmembers in the scene. The stage directions are in capitals and none of the characters' names are underlined because in this scene they're all already on the stage. We also see how stage directions within dialogue are not indented on a separate line like in a feature script and also are capitalized.

With all the extra spacing and the fact that multi-cam shows often have more dialogue and jokes, multi-cam scripts can be longer than those for single-camera sitcoms. Often, multi-cam scripts are about 40 pages long. Some *Seinfeld* scripts were as long as 50 pages because of the rapid fire jokes.

❓ No FIGS

And, when listing the scenes there's a rule called *No FIGS*. They skip over scenes F, I, G and S. Probably because those letters look too much like other ones. So, a script might have SCENE E followed by SCENE H, then SCENE J, etc.

Single-Camera Scripts

Single-camera shows are much simpler, and their formatting resembles film scripts in many ways. They can utilize many locations, devices like flashbacks, cut-aways, and dream sequences, and don't rely on having so many jokes per page, like multi-camera shows do. If the show is meant for a platform without commercials, it's still broken into acts, but they don't list scenes. There can still be teasers, cold opens, and tags, but the stage directions within and outside of dialogue are formatted the way they would be for films.

From *The Andy Griffith Show* to *Doogie Howser, M.D.* to *30 Rock* to *The Office* to *Modern Family* to *Veep* to *The Goldbergs*, single-cam shows can have many more scenes, quicker scenes, and aren't shot before a live audience. They are also usually about 30-35 pages long.

Here's an example from *Parks and Recreation:*

```
                        ACT ONE

VT: SERIES OF SWEEPING SHOTS OF FAMOUS
LANDMARKS

We see shots of famous political images --
the Capitol Building, floor of the Senate,
a recent Presidential inauguration, the
White House, Mount Rushmore, etc.

                  LESLIE (V.O.)
        I love politics. I've always loved
        politics. "The game."
```

```
            B-Roll: SLOW PAN OVER some BOOKSHELVES.
            Nothing but Political biographies.


                         LESLIE (CONT'D)
                    Some people say that politics is
                    show business for ugly people.   I
                    disagree. It's show business for
                    real people -- people whose talents
                    aren't dancing and singing, but
                    rather talking and talking.

            INT. LESLIE'S OFFICE - DAY


            ANGLE ON: a framed copy of the
            Constitution... a portrait of Thomas
            Jefferson...
```

As you can see, there is no scene list, and the camera can be used in more ways than in multi-camera scripts.

Single-cam scripts can use voice-overs, such as in *Black-ish, The Office, Parks and Recreation,* and *Modern Family,* to name a few. They might also use a device known as *talking heads*, where characters break the fourth wall and speak directly to camera. Here's another example from *Parks and Recreation*:

```
                         JOE
                    (to himself, proudly) Still got it,
                    Joe.


                         LESLIE (O.C.)
                    No, you don't.

            TOM TALKING HEAD


                         TOM
                    All of Joe's lines are sewage
                    related. "If you've got a clogged
                    drain, I'll bring the snake." "Got
                    any sewage on you? Would you like
                    some?" And my favorite: "I'd like
                    to lie face down in your gutter."
                    Yeah. He said that. To a human
                    being.

            EXT. CITY HALL - LATER


            Chris does DEEP KNEE BENDS and SQUATS
            outside the door.
```

With the many differences between content, overall guidelines, and formatting of single- and multi-camera shows, it's a good idea to study them in-depth.

When giving notes on a TV pilot, we Readers should know these rules, so we can know how to market the project, determine whether it's a format our bosses are looking for, and see if it has been formatted correctly. These questions are all a part of the Craft/Technical/Presentation category in our coverage.

The Magical Mystical Creature: The TV Pilot

Now that we know about platforms, length, and formatting how do we assess a *pilot* (the first episode of an original show)?

Writers who want a staff job on an existing show must write an original pilot and Readers must assess them. Some prestigious competitions like the Warner Bros. and Disney require *spec* scripts (samples of already successful shows), but mostly Readers read pilots.

Feature films must establish characters and worlds, include conflicts, and follow structural, genre and all the other rules and guidelines we talked about earlier, but a pilot must do even more. It must set up the same things as a feature script *and* define what the series will be about week after week and season after season. No matter the platform, a pilot needs to have enough plots, subplots, conflicts, and stories to seem profitable, fit with the platform's brand (if they have one), and prove that it can attract enough eyeballs for however long the series runs.

Pilots need to hook the Reader with something major right away, and set up future episodes, character, season, and series arcs (usually in a *pitch deck* or document that Readers may or may not see.) We see these more often for dramas than sitcoms.

In one-hour shows the pilot needs to set up the world, characters, and situation, without throwing exposition at us, and write a great story. We should become immersed in that episode, and either be satisfied by the resolution and want to watch more (like with procedurals) or end on a cliffhanger so we *have to see* what happens next (like serialized shows).

Questions I often address in coverage of pilots are whether it fits with a specific platform, has good act breaks (if applicable), sets up what the series will be about, and has strong writing, characters, and dialogue. We must be hooked, know that this has a market, is "familiar yet different", addresses some sort of current issue or demand, and follows the guidelines and rules of the categories previously discussed in this book.

When reading pilots, I often see an intriguing "A" plot, but not enough subplots. In that case I may recommend setting up future conflicts, relationships, and subplots for recurring characters. These can provide more fodder for later episodes and seasons to come. It's not enough to have a funny husband in a sitcom; a show should also establish future storylines for the wife, nosy neighbor, high school kid, etc.

TV or Not TV? That Is the Question

When assessing scripts, I sometimes come across a feature that might work better as a TV show, or a TV pilot that might work better as a movie. This might be due to the scale, audience, and longevity of the project.

For example, if I read something in a competition, perhaps the writer has written it as a feature and I suggest it might make a better TV show. This could be bad news if they don't agree with me or are defensive in general, or good news, because:

- TV might be an obvious market that they didn't consider.
- The project may make more money as a TV show because it can span a larger and longer-lasting universe.
- It's a competition, so they can still adjust it before sending it out.

If, however, they were submitting a TV show to ABC and I deemed it a movie, I'm telling them it's a no-go for that network. Or, it may be a dead end if they submit a feature to a film production company that doesn't do TV. Either way, they're submitting it in one format, but the Reader believes it would be better in a different one. When reading for a company that does both TV and movies, if we report that the script may work better as something else, the higher-ups will understand that it needs more work before they consider it.

When should we recommend such a change? A movie script may work better as a TV show if it won't draw in a huge theatrical audience, feels more intimate than a movie, or seems more like a set-up for exploring future plots and worlds. Conversely, if a TV script doesn't seem like it can sustain many episodes or seasons then maybe it's time to recommend re-jiggering it as a feature film. I often read feature scripts about cops and find myself wondering, "With so many cop shows over the years, why would people pay money to go to a theater to watch cops? Why should this story be on the big screen?"

A Reader's ability to discern if a project is right for TV vs. film will develop over time. Why is *Superman* a movie but *Supergirl* a show? Is it about gender? *Wonder Woman* was once a show and now it's a movie. *Captain Marvel* is a movie, but *Batgirl* is a show. So were *Arrow* and *The Flash*. Yet *Spiderman* is a movie (over and over again). Is it D.C. Comics vs. Marvel? *Justice League* was a movie and *Agents of S.H.I.E.L.D.* was a show. Is it costumes? Is there a nostalgia element since *Wonder Woman, Superman, Batman,* and *The Incredible Hulk* were shows back in the 60's, 70s and 80's?

Companies want certain things at certain times, and often chase the last great hit. Learn the current trends. With the advent of Disney+, HBO Max, and Covid, big screen movies were made available on streaming services due to global conditions and deals. As time goes on, we'll see how that affects the industry.

To recap: TV has different rules based on format, length, platform, and the times. Be familiar with them all. Watch a lot. Read the news of the industry and of the world. Know the markets — not just for different platforms, but also if companies want to reach international markets as well. (A funny documentary to watch is *Exporting Raymond* where we see Phil Rosenthal navigating and adapting his show, *Everybody Loves Raymond,* for a Russian audience.)

Writers should write what they're passionate about but also know the market. Readers should know that all companies will have their basic mandates ("We're looking for our version of *Game of Thrones...*" "We promote diversity..." "Our demographic is 60-death," etc.) But all will say they want "good stories," intriguing worlds, and compelling characters. Hopefully that will never change.

Exercises

1. If a comedy writer was writing a half-hour pilot, what are at least three considerations they'd weigh before deciding if they should write a multi-camera sitcom or a single-camera sitcom? (Consider format, tone, market, type of humor, how long it could go on for, various devices, and such).

2. Look at the following (made up) loglines. Decide whether each project should be a feature film, a one-hour show, or a half-hour show? Explain why. Remember, some of these may feel like they could be more than one format. You might need more information. In that case, explain what might make it good for the different types.

   For example, if I say, "Four friends buy a roller rink," it sounds like a workplace TV sitcom. However, if they buy a haunted roller rink, depending on tone and content, it could be a comedy or drama, and perhaps even a TV series or a feature film.

   A. After her husband has been kidnapped, an agoraphobic woman has four days to locate him before he is killed.

   B. Sick of adulting, a recent college graduate moves in with his grumpy grandfather.

   C. A newspaper reporter in the 1970's goes missing and body parts with a killer's demands show up in different places.

    D.   After losing his wife, a reckless man joins the army and is sent to the Middle East to join its explosives unit.

3. Whether from memory or with the help of the internet, identify the following (and don't use any of my examples in this chapter):

    A.   A one-hour TV show that dealt with a recurring world or theme but a changed cast or focus each season.

    B.   A multi-camera family sitcom.

    C.   A single camera family sitcom.

    D.   A workplace sitcom either single-camera or multi-camera.

    E.   A one-hour TV show where someone solves a different case week after week.

    F.   A one-hour dramedy.

    G.   A cable show with fewer than 13 episodes per season.

    H.   A broadcast family drama.

    I.   A TV show that was turned into a movie.

    J.   A movie that was adapted into a TV show.

16

Books

Diamonds in the Rough

The Oscars have two categories for screenwriting: Best Original Screenplay and Best Adapted Screenplay. The latter is for screenplays that came from previously established material such as short stories, plays, articles, and, of course, books. *Schindler's List, Forrest Gump, A Beautiful Mind, Slumdog Millionaire, Precious, The Social Network, 12 Years a Slave, Moonlight, BlacKkKlansman, The Lord of the Rings* movies, and many more were all adapted from books.

What Are They Looking For?

An agent, production company, or network might throw lots of books at their Readers (so duck), because they love already-established brands and content. In fact, many screenwriters start by writing a book first, knowing that strangely enough, the book could generate interest in a screenplay adaptation.

Studios and production companies scour bestseller lists and scramble to get the rights to books, so they'll often ask Readers to cover hot titles and assess whether or not the studio should grab them before others do.

And, as with screenplays, some books are sent to execs (possibly as an unpublished manuscript or a self-published book) who will want to know if it has potential or not. Specifically, executives want *to know if the book could/should be adapted into a movie or TV show.*

Don't Worry About Structure

Books are very different than screenplays or teleplays. They're much longer so many of the rules for film and television do not apply. One page does not equal one minute of screen time. Books rarely conform to three-act structure, they can have more characters, subplots, 50-page digressions, and so on. Therefore, when writing coverage on a book, Readers aren't expected to analyze it in the same way as a script in terms of structure or formatting.

Now, one may ask, "Couldn't anyone find something in any book?" For example, the book may be boring, but on page 12 there's a fun little space-doggie who plays the harmonica. Why not option the book and just take that part? That could happen. But it usually doesn't.

Just like with scripts, a book should have a good story, world, premise, character, relationship, message, or experience. Since the author themselves — or more likely a different screenwriter — will need to adapt it, Readers can suggest a *possible* framework for an adaptation.

Suppose a book is a lovely memoir involving a fascinating character who tells their fascinating thoughts about going camping. We might suggest that an adaptation explore the camping trip, but frame and focus on the story, main character, goal, obstacle, and resolution within.

A Reader doesn't have to figure out what the actual structure would be. They can simply suggest elements that could be the focus of a screenplay.

While the Reader's job is to assess if there's something in the book that could make a lot of money, attract talent, and get critical acclaim, sometimes the boss already knows the answer because they might have already bought the rights or even read it themselves.

Where's the Beef?

Imagine writing coverage on an 800-page book about Elvis. The adapted screenplay can't include everything in those 800 pages, so the screenwriter must find the protagonist-driven feature film take that's hiding inside. Coverage of that book should state whether there is enough of a protagonist-based story within the book and suggest what it might be.

Any time a company acquires a book and wants to adapt it they bring in different screenwriters to pitch their "take." (Unless the company plans to use the original author or has an A-list writer in mind.) How would they adapt it? I did this for a director and since the book they were considering was based on a historical (and mystical) person, there was a lot of room for different approaches. Readers must consider how to turn the book into a feature film since film audiences are different from book audiences and need a more proactive and focused story.

A great example of a movie changing a lot from the original book (and boy was I disappointed and surprised) is *A Beautiful Mind*. I saw the movie and was so excited that this woman stayed with this difficult man for so long and then, was sad to discover that in the book (and real life) she didn't. The screenwriter also cut a lot of anti-Semitism from the book.

❓ What Is a Book Option?

Screenplays and books can be bought, but they can also be *optioned*, a type of sale that is more frequent with books. When something is optioned, usually an amount of money is given to the writer, and the person optioning the book has a certain amount of time to get the project completed. ("I will option this book for a one-year period for $1000"). At the end of the option period, the option might get sold which will net the writer more money. However, if nothing comes of the option, at the end of the option period it can either be renewed, or else the deal is over and the rights return to the writer (who gets to keep the option money). Think of it as renting the right to sell it, versus actually selling it.

What If It Sucks but a Famous Person Wrote It or Is Attached?

If the world's most famous musician, actor, actress, director, author, or influencer writes a book — or is already attached to a book someone else wrote — that spells money and a built-in fan base. This is something Readers have to consider. Just like with screenplays, we must see if a book fits a company's brand, mandate, need for accolades, or has talent attached. We might be reading a book by an ex-president that doesn't go anywhere, but they did — so we might recommend it.

Hollywood is full of tales of producers launching their careers by getting their hands on an important book and optioning it — thereby controlling the rights. Example: Robert Evans purchased the rights to the 1966 book *The Detective*, which was made into a film starring Frank Sinatra, Lee Remick, Jack Klugman, Robert Duvall, and Jacqueline Bisset in 1968. He also got the rights to a paltry lesser-known book: *The Godfather*, which at the time was an unfinished 60-page manuscript called *Mafia*. The option was for $12,500. If studios want the book, they must go through the producers that control the rights — *and attach them to the project*. In this case, the attachment of Robert Evans, an unknown producer at that time, did not make the project more marketable.

Big attachments can make a project more desirable, and many people have attached themselves to books to make *themselves* more desirable. As with all projects, if a book has name recognition, that should be taken into consideration and we might give it a *recommend* or *consider* as opposed to a *pass*.

Mo' Reading, Mo' Money

When Readers are hired to write coverage of books, there's one negative and many more positives. For example, if they're reading a 500-page book that's bad, because reading it will take longer. But on the other hand, if it's great… they're lucky because most companies pay Readers more to write coverage for books. So, in a best-case scenario they might get to read a good book *and* earn more money.

Another positive: the coverage isn't much longer than for a screenplay. When I've written coverage for books, I've had to write longer synopses, but the comment section stayed the same. If it was a long book or manuscript, I might read 50 pages, summarize that, read the next 50 pages, summarize that, and so on. The coverage was the same, the money was better, and I enjoyed a nice book.

Exercises

This is a three-part exercise:

1. **Read a book, short story or novel that was adapted into a movie**. Be sure to choose a movie you haven't seen. Before going on, write a short "Comments section" about how you think it should be adapted into a feature. What should the focus be, what should or should not be included or added, and how might the book be turned into a protagonist-driven three-act feature?

2. **Read the screenplay.** See if the screenwriter adapted it the way you thought it should be done. What was used, what was discarded? How was it reframed and refocused? And subjectively, which did you like better (the book or the screenplay) and why? Also, what were the different feelings you had in reading each one? Which engaged you more?

3. **Watch the film.** It most likely will change more from book to script, but remembering the book, note what made it to the film and what didn't. Not everything from the script makes it into the film and you already saw what made it from the book to the script. So now ask yourself what you think they got "right" and "wrong"? How do you feel subjectively — like a fan of the book might feel — and how do you feel objectively about the book vs. film?

17

How to Give Notes

'Tis Better to Give Than to Receive

There is an art and a craft to writing notes. Bosses want coverage written in a specific way and with a certain amount of professionalism, objectivity, and tact but not all writers are great at receiving notes, so Readers need to write with care for their feelings.

Earlier in this book, I addressed how to assess the tone of *a script,* but now it's time to talk about our own tone. Readers must consider who their audience is, know what they want to say, and remember that their notes must be crystal clear.

Notes for a Writer

This is where a Reader must be their most sensitive because the writer who wrote the script will read the notes themselves. They regard the Reader as an expert and pay for their help and guidance.

Snowflakes and Sensitivity (It Protects *You*)

Readers should write coverage with the most sensitive of snowflakes in mind. This does not mean you should write things like, "Good for you! Yay! Everyone gets a trophy!" Instead, err on the side of being sensitive for three reasons:

First, some writers are sensitive. They hired us to *help them*. They put their art and self-expression into our hands, asking, "How do I improve it?" Our job is to answer that request respectfully. Never say, "Don't. Keep your day job." They're going for a dream so help them. And for me, that means *acknowledging what works and offering guidance on what doesn't.*

Second, A Reader should encourage or help because the companies they work for offer *a service*. Readers aren't hired to kill their clients' dreams. They represent the company, so the rules of customer service apply. Just like a salesperson in retail shouldn't say, "Honey, you can't pull off those jeans," Readers shouldn't say, "Dearie, you can't pull off this profession."

And third, some writers can be defensive. So being sensitive *to them* protects *the Reader*. Not everyone can take notes or will agree with ours, so don't give them ammunition to kvetch or complain.

Coverage services and competitions will deal with writers' comments, complaints, and quirks that their Readers never hear about. But occasionally, since they are a business, they may forward those comments to us and ask us to address them. Writers' comments on coverage can range from hostile to delusional to totally justified. Remember, we're writing our thoughts on a document, and they will interpret that. (This is why we must be clear in our notes).

If we come across something offensive, our coverage notes probably won't change the perspective of a writer who's been thinking this way all their life. If we tell them that something in their script is racist, agist, homophobic, or sexist they may get defensive.

While many things are objectively offensive, some may be subjective. Not everyone is offended by similar things. For example, one could cover the pilot of HBO's *Euphoria* and say, "There are too many references to drugs," but some Readers would know that the targeted audience would disagree. So, the first step is to see if the script truly is offensive or if the script is meant for a specific audience.

If you believe the script is objectively offensive then you must explain the problem from the prospective of executives or audiences. For example, I might address something "objectively offensive" this way:

> In today's current climate, executives may not be too receptive to overtly chauvinistic or racist characters.

And yes, it's different if they're telling the story of a neo-Nazi who ends up in jail for their racist crimes. There are and will be numerous offensive characters and worlds — but that's different from the *writer or project* coming across as offensive. Consider the 1970's TV show, *All in the Family*. It was about a bigot but did not promote bigotry.

Speak to what the writer hopes to achieve (a sale) rather than to their morals.

The Ouch Factor

Whether a script is good or not, the writer has expressed their thoughts and feelings, and has taken a chance. We should guide and not dissuade them; be sensitive in our tone and notes just in case. And there are some small tips that I use that may help.

Words like *no* and *none* can be harsh. So here are some words I pepper in: *seems, some, more, better, a bit, a little, further, might*. I also point to the result they're going for.

Look at the difference here:

> There is no plot.

I might instead write:

> The plot seems a bit unfocused.

The first suggests that the writer has failed while the second lets them know that there's room for improvement.

I might also give a note such as:

> The main character's goal could clearer.

Even if it's not clear at all, this at least suggests that there's something to work with.

Look at the difference between these two statements:

> The characters are flat and have no redeeming qualities.

> We'd love to know more about the characters, in order to understand their motivations better.

Saying that we want *more* suggests that something *is* there and the writer should go further. Also, I like to explain what the suggestion *will achieve*, because it's easier for writers to take a note when we remind them about their overall goal: to sell the script, to get the film made, for audiences to understand their vision, care about their story, etc.

I also recommend starting with the strengths or what works, and then detail what doesn't. This doesn't mean spending a lot of time praising them or pointing out all the things that work, just a few will suffice. The writer hired us to help them make their script better so a litany of praise doesn't help them. However, they may want to know that some things are good, so we state that right away. Addressing what works first will calm down the insecure, deactivate the defensive, and make it easier for them to hear what doesn't work afterwards.

Note that, if I have a private consult or know the person, I'll adapt to their experience and comfort levels.

I personally have never received hostile reactions or feedback from writers. Usually if my company tells me a writer reached out about their coverage it's to get clarification on a note. And in my private and personal consults I'm often told to just "rip the band-aid off" and tell them what isn't working. However, many clients have told me disconcerting stories of other feedback or coverage experiences. I've heard a few say, "I don't think they even read my script!" Or the writers really disagreed with the notes, thought they were incoherent, subjective, mean, unprofessional, and in a few cases, that the Reader had no idea what they were doing.

Be Explicit

I want to reiterate what I said about being clear in our notes, since the writer can misinterpret or misunderstand what Readers write in coverage and they will not get a chance to explain or clarify themselves.

For example, if I write something like:

> The protagonist needs more agency.

They might not know what I mean. It's more clear to say something like:

> What are the stakes for the protagonist to achieve their goal? What are the consequences if they don't? Right now, it isn't fully clear, and specifics can help inform character and aid the audience in better identifying with and emotionally investing in the protagonist's journey.

Not only do more people know what stakes and consequences are as opposed to a word like "agency," I'm also focusing on the effect and outcome that writers want.

I also recommend that we don't write in first person and avoid the words *I* or *me*. Here are some words I use: *we, readers, executives, an audience*, or I just take out all pronouns. Not only do I sound more professional, but it's harder for the writer to get defensive.

Compare these two lines:

> I think the first act drags on a bit.

> The first act has to propel an audience into the second act with a high-stakes, protagonist-driven goal already underway.

Besides the fact that the second comment is smarter, I often refer to an audience or an executive because a defensive writer might think I statements are just my opinion. I'm reminding them who they're writing for, what the effect may be, and that I represent a potential buyers and audiences.

Also, don't talk directly to the writer. Don't use the word *you*. Stating the notes rather than "having a conversation with the writer" is more professional. For example, instead of writing:

> You need to activate the protagonist by the end of Act One.

It could be:

> The protagonist could be more active by the end of Act One.

Our job is to improve their script, not make it our own. There is no truth — only suggestions. We can nudge, suggest, recommend, etc. Notes should put writers on a path to their own discovery, not ours.

Let's say that there's a flat character with no arc and her name is Judy. We might want to say, "Judy is a flat character" but instead we offer, "Judy's character can use further development," or "We want to know more about Judy to understand the stakes of her goal."

Maybe we have an idea about how to move the story forward. We could say: "In order to have Judy drive the love story, she could take some action. One example might be to tattoo her name on Manny's arm. This, or something like it, would make her more active." Offer an example and focus on *why* something like that is needed, as opposed to telling them *what to do*.

No One Cares About Your Favorite Films

Sometimes new Readers will allude to other films or TV shows in order to aid the writer, and while this can be helpful, it has to be done for the right reasons and in a specific way to protect both the Reader and the writer.

Don't try to impress people with a vast knowledge about film and TV. Many people are simply mad about certain films and shows, and drop references because they really like them, want to impress the writer, or are full of knowledge and good intentions. Too many of these can sound like name-dropping. Also, they may not have heard of the film or show, might hate it, or totally disagree with the comparison.

However, we can allude to an *element* of another project as a teachable lesson (if we're not condescending or too much of an obsessed fan of said project). For example, I often read scripts that don't have a lot going on and then at the end have a big reveal and think that this will make up for all that didn't come before. I might write, "Consider a movie like *The Sixth Sense*. Without the ending, it stands on its own, with a clear, protagonist-driven plot, and then a revelation that adds additional layers." I'm referring to an *aspect* of the film so, whether the writer likes that film or not, or hasn't seen or heard of it, I'm pointing out what that film accomplishes successfully, and how the writer might learn from that element.

I would never write: "You know what you should see? *Nomadland. Minari. Judas and the Black Messiah*." This is pompous, mean, and nothing but a list of things. (Also, bonus points for noticing that I spoke directly to the writer).

Notes for the Executive

Remember, coverage for writers focuses more on comments than synopses. Executives don't need as many comments, since the script can always be rewritten — they mainly want the nuts and bolts. And while we should always be professional in how we give notes to executives (and many of my tips still apply), we don't have to be *as* sensitive as when writing coverage for a writer.

Tone

While we don't have to be as gentle with executives as with a writer, we do need to sound professional, objective, and tactful. The point is to tell the executive the story in the synopsis, and then give our assessment in the comment section, especially since the synopsis can't tell them how well the story was told.

I still don't ever use *I*, *we*, or *you* — especially not *you* since it's not going to the writer. And I can pepper in some *seems like, possibly, more, better*, etc. But perhaps not as much. I'm not in jeopardy of dealing with a sensitive, delicate, or defensive writer.

Less Sensitive, But Don't Be a Bitter Writer

Coverage isn't a book report, but it is a report of sorts. We must report the story and report the potential, and leave our career goals out. Do not write in the comments to an executive:

> This sci-fi fantasy pales in comparison to MY opus:
> *Mars, Venus and Saturn: An Unexpected Throuple.*

> Now, that script is a brilliant deep dive into man and
> woman and man's search for meaning in a universe
> grown cold…

Maintain an upbeat, professional tone, and stay objective. Network some other time. Connect to all bosses and coworkers in person, and not on the page. They don't want to be bothered by a Reader's career goals, hear them unprofessionally gush, or feel a lot of negative energy and attitude coming from the way they give notes. Readers can state what needs work or doesn't work, but they shouldn't convey how much *they'd* love to steal the writer's job.

We're Their Eyes and Ears

Remember our purpose: We are the executive's eyes and ears. Our job is to reduce their workload. Instead of reading 4000 (100+ page) scripts, they read 4000 coverage reports. The coverage must inform them of the main story — including any weird devices, time jumps and so on — in a way they can comprehend. And the comments must let them know how well this was executed. We may tell them the story of the TV pilot *Pen15*, but the hook needs to be conveyed in the comment section, of how the 30-something writers will play middle school kids among actual middle school kids.

We can tell them that *Insecure* is about an insecure African-American woman and her friends and the funny plot and subplots in the pilot, but the comments will tell them how smart the dialogue is, how refreshing the world and characters are, how well the humor works, etc.

If Readers comment on characters or elements that they didn't mention in the synopsis, either go back and insert a mention there, or else describe and introduce them in the comments and state how they help or hinder the main story.

Should They Buy It? Make It? Rep the Writer?

The comments for a writer focus on how to make the script better. The comments for agents are: should they represent the writer, is this a good project for one of their clients, or, if this is a new work by an existing client, then know that these are notes that a writer may read. In all scenarios, the Reader should know if they are looking for big studio pictures, character-driven works, or something specific.

If an agent represents a director or actor (basically "talent"), a Reader must assess if the script is a good fit for that client. What the agent wants may be somewhere in that script's story but overall, the agent wants to know if the script should be considered for a particular actor or director.

An agent may want coverage for a script from a writer that they already represent. Sometimes an agent asks for coverage on a client's script and then gives the notes verbally to the client as if it came from them, but that's usually not the case. Most often, the coverage is for the agent, but the writer may also read it. Don't be *in*sensitive, but don't worry about being as cautious as when hired to help green writers.

Again, in coverage for executives don't use *I* or *me* or address the exec directly. Instead of writing, "You will love the funny lines on page 6." say, "The dialogue in the date scene on page 6 is really funny."

For offensive material talk about the intended goal — that this will sell, get made, be viewed, and become a success. So perhaps say, "Some audience members might get offended by the dialogue on page 6…"

Agents Can Always Order Rewrites

Unlike competitions, agents and executives aren't assessing a script in its current form as the final product. They know that the script can be rewritten, so it doesn't have to be perfect. However, Readers shouldn't focus on giving specifics on how a rewrite should be done in the comments. Instead state the script's various strengths and weaknesses. It isn't our job to guide the writer into improving it, it's about noting the areas that work and those that don't.

We Have No Idea If They Know Someone with a Football Field Full of Marijuana

Movies get made for different reasons. Years ago, my friend answered an ad to edit (and ended up directing) a movie in Europe, where a man had a football field-sized crop of marijuana and wanted to make a movie so he could include it. That was the whole reason for making the film, and the whole story had to be crafted around — and in service of — that marijuana field.

We might *pass* on a script for an agent without knowing that their client wants to do a movie that has a hairless cat in it because they just got a hairless cat. Or more realistically, perhaps a client or company has done one kind of project and wants to branch out?

The point is, when giving notes we'll always give our professional opinion based on the art, the craft, the marketability, and the elements we've gone over (characters, worlds, story, structure, etc.) but at the end of the day there might be unknown factors at play in determining whether the script gets made.

Chapter 17 | How to Give Notes 167

Exercises

1. Look at the following notes. See if you can spot what might not work and some ways that you could change it. Remember as Readers we're professional, so write in the third person, and be sensitive and constructive. Guide and support, and be nice and clear.

   A.   The second act is boring.

   B.   I don't understand why kids in Compton have British accents.

   C.   The stakes could be higher. Have Slav like two girls and must decide between them.

   D.   While your characters are colorful and fun, they could be further developed.

2. Here are three possible scenarios one might encounter as a Reader. How would you handle them? Be honest.

   A.   You work for a very successful TV agent. You are given a TV pilot that is subpar and poorly written — and you have a very similar pilot you wrote that is much better and stronger.

   B.   You receive a script to read from a coverage service and spend many hours reading and meticulously crafting professional, thoughtful, and constructive notes for the screenwriter. The company sends you an email saying, "The writer has a few questions and complaints. They don't agree with a lot of your notes and think that you didn't read it fully, and want you to redo the coverage."

   C.   You read a TV pilot for a cable network or streaming platform that has a lot of sex and sexual depictions. In the beginning, you think nothing, but then a few of the depictions start to trigger or disturb you. You know your company likes "edgy" fare, but your Spidey sense indicates that something is off.

18

Receiving Coverage

Looking at Samples, Both as
Writer and as an Executive

I'd now like to give both Readers and writers the experience of what it feels like to receive coverage. In the next two sections I will provide some excerpts and samples. For each, I'll state who you are (your job/position/title) so you can read from that POV. What do you notice?

Reading from the POV of a Writer

Imagine that you are a writer. You paid for coverage. You hope your script is good and want to know how to make it better. You're looking for coverage that is clear, concise, helpful, sensitive, and professional.

Here's an excerpt of the coverage you receive:

> The story is a very lean, well-paced narrative. Everything is coherent and clearly depicts every characters issue and their relationship with one another. However, the entire story feels aimless with no clear protagonist, hero's journey or

> structural beats. While there is a ramp up in the stakes as we approach the end, the characters feel confined to an episodic journey that leads to an abrupt ending. It feels as if we're watching a very long TV pilot that will explore potential story threads later.

How do you feel? Do you understand what they're saying? Do you feel you got useful direction? Do you feel confused, discouraged, inspired, or helped? Is it professional with no mistakes?

"Characters" is missing an apostrophe. Notes like "the entire story seems aimless" may be very negative and daunting, and the list of how there is "*no* clear protagonist, journey, or structural beats", goes against my rule of tact. And while I've said that some scripts may work better as TV pilots, there is a way to offer opinions that more constructively. Also, I see no suggestions or guidance. Many writers may feel a bit crushed rather than aided and inspired.

Now look at another example:

> Whilst this script hit many of the marks it should have and is written clearly and, in a way, suited to the story, a producer reading many scripts a week might feel this is a 'paint by numbers script'. The biggest issue was that it had no real character change, and it was hard to work out who the main character actually was.

Telling someone they have a "paint by numbers" script may sound a little tactless and some writers might not even understand what that means. They conclude this note in a tactless and uninspiring way. It may leave the writer feeling badly and wondering how to fix their script.

Some of you are tougher and may think the above note is fine, but not everyone will. If you paid for notes to help you improve your script, what would this excerpt leave you thinking and feeling?

Another good exercise is to rewrite these excerpts in a more clear, professional, and helpful way. For example, I might redo the previous one this way:

> The plot points are there, and the story is pretty strong, but it may need to go deeper in order to differentiate it more and to add a slightly larger hook. The main character's arc could be stronger. Set up their strengths and flaws early on, track their arc throughout, and by the end make it clear how they grew, changed, healed, confronted, or accepted what they needed to. Also, at times the different

> characters and stories compete for focus. In Act
> One it feels as if it's X's story, and then in Act Two
> Y gets more screen time.

And how would you feel receiving these notes?

> This an action-packed David verses Goliath tale.
> The action is fast with extensive directors'
> details/notes. There are high stakes for all principals
> with life or death outcomes. The concerns present
> themselves in clarity of the storyline for the first part
> of the script which is impacted by the action and
> flashbacks. The format presents a bit of a challenge
> and you may want to look at other software or
> examples as comparisons.

This note describes what the script's strengths are but is it clearly written and presented? First, would everyone know what directors' details or notes are? This usually implies that a lot of camera angles are included in the script, or that all the scenes are numbered in preparation for shooting the film. Second, the line that begins with, "The concerns…" ironically addresses clarity in writing but is unclear itself. And third, what if the writer was a professional? Would they want to be told to look at screenwriting software? And finally, by the end of these notes would you really understand the specifics of what's wrong or have a clear vision of what you need to do for a rewrite?

Reading from the POV of an Executive

Now imagine that you are not a perfect, gorgeous, sensitive, defensive, seasoned, or new writer. You're an executive. Or maybe an agent, a development executive at a production company, a TV executive, or similar. Remember that you are reading coverage to help you decide whether or not to read the script yourself. Synopses are very important in this case and so are the comment sections.

The following are coverage samples that some of my students wrote, for projects that we already know were made. Some of you may have seen or read these projects, if so pretend that you haven't.

But now, you are a big literary agent in a fancy-shmancy agency. You receive a feature script named *Carol*. Your assistant covered it and sent this coverage to you. It's got attachments, by the way. As an agent, you're wondering if you should rep the writer and/or this project. Can you understand the story based on the synopsis? What about the comments? Do they help you get a sense of the script? At the end, you'll see the Reader's recommendation as to whether you should pass, consider, or they recommend it. Do you agree?

FANCY SHMANCY AGENCY

Title: CAROL

Writer: Phyllis Nagy

Studio: The Weinstein Company

Prod Company: Number 9 Films, Film4, Killer Films

Producers: Elizabeth Karlsen, Stephen Woolley, Christine Vachon

Draft Date: N/A

Pages: 115

Genre: Romantic drama

Time: 1952-1953

Location: New York City

Reader: XXX

Date: 10/27/2020

LOGLINE:

A young aspiring female photographer and an older, elegant woman form a romantic relationship in 1952 New York City and must face the consequences of their relationship in a world that doesn't accept them.

PREMISE:

(No ages given)

It's the holiday season in New York City, 1952. THERESE BELIVET is a salesclerk at Frankenberg's Toy Department where her boyfriend, RICHARD SEMCO also works. Therese first spots CAROL AIRD browsing dolls. Therese convinces Carol to buy her daughter, RINDY a train set for Christmas. When Carol leaves, Therese realizes that she left a glove behind. Instead of being excited about a European trip Richard is trying to plan, Therese is more concerned with returning Carol's glove. They end up getting lunch together and Carol invites Therese over next Sunday.

Carol's lawyer FRED HAMES tells her that HARGE, her husband, has sought an injunction which denies Carol any access to Rindy until the court hearing. He wants sole custody of Rindy. Infuriated, Carol decides to spend that time going West, and she wants Therese to join her. When they make it to Ohio, Therese meets TOMMY TUCKER, a seemingly nice young man. When they get down the road and get a flat tire, it is none other than Tommy of who stops to help them repair it. They make it to Iowa and Carol and Therese finally kiss and make love for the first time! The next morning, they discover Tommy

Tucker works for Harge and he videotaped/recorded their affair the night before. On the way back home Carol leaves with nothing but a note for Therese saying that they can't see each other again.

Back from the road trip, Therese gets a position at *The New York Times*. Carol meets with Harge, Fred, and Harge's lawyer, JERRY RIX. Carol has been seeing a psychotherapist to help her overcome her homosexuality so she can be a more fit mother for Rindy. She says that she wants her daughter but admits that she wanted what happened with Therese. She decides to give Harge permanent custody with regular visitation, so they don't mess their daughter's life up.

Carol meets up with Therese, tells her she loves her and would like to live with her, but Therese declines. Carol invites her to dinner, and Therese declines that too. But in the end, Therese shows up and takes Carol up on her offer.

SYNOPSIS:
New York City, 1953. JACK TAFT (late 20s) runs into his friend THERESE BELIVET speaking with CAROL AIRD. Carol goes home and Therese takes Jack up on his offer to go to their friend, Phil's for a party. Therese flirts with GENEVIEVE CANTRELL at Phil's party.

Jump back to 1952 in the Frankenberg's Toy Department during Christmas time. Therese works as a temp salesclerk. Her boyfriend, RICHARD SEMCO also works there. Therese spots Carol for the first time browsing dolls and ultimately convinces her to purchase a train set for her daughter. When Carol goes, she accidentally leaves her glove behind.

Flash forward to 1953 briefly, Therese arrives at PHIL MCELROY's apartment and sees Phil's brother / their friend, DANNIE. Dannie works at *The New York Times*.

Back to 1952, Richard has big plans of taking Therese to France, but she is unexcited about it. Dannie invites Therese to come check out *The New York Times*. Maybe she could take pictures for them one day. Dannie kisses Therese during her visit at *The Times*.

Therese mails Carol's glove to her with a note. Despite Carol throwing away the letter, she calls Therese at work and invites her to lunch. They start to get to know each other, and Carol invites her to her place on Sunday. She also discloses that she and her husband, Harge are getting a divorce.

Carol's best friend, ABBY picks her up and takes her to a get-together at CY HARRISON's house, Harge's boss. Carol feels underdressed as she arrives. HARGE wants Carol to spend Christmas with him at his parents', but she doesn't want to.

Carol and Therese head to Carol's on Sunday and pick up a Christmas tree on the way. Therese plays the piano while Carol wraps the train set under the tree. The two women have a moment when Carol grazes Therese's shoulder right before

Harge drunkenly bursts in saying he is going to take RINDY for Christmas Eve. They get into an argument and Harge is confused why Therese is there. He ends up taking Rindy for the holiday.

Carol goes to FRED HAMES's law office; he tells her that Harge has sought an injunction which denies Carol any access to Rindy until the custody hearing on the basis of her "immoral" relationship with Abby in the past. He wants sole custody of Rindy. Carol decides she is going to spend that time going West, and she wants Therese to join. Richard is upset that Therese is spending her money on this trip instead of the European trip they were going to take together. Therese heads to Carol's and stays in her guest room. The next morning, Therese meets Abby before she and Carol head out on their big road trip.

When Carol and Therese make it to Canton, Ohio, Therese meets a young man at the ice machine, TOMMY TUCKER. On New Year's Eve, they get a flat tire. They wave down a passing car for help, and it is none other than Tommy Tucker. He repairs the tire for them. They make it to Iowa and Carol and Therese finally kiss and make love for the first time! Just when everything seems to be falling into place, Carol receives a telegram the next morning. It's not good news. Carol grabs her gun from her suitcase and bursts into the room next door where Tommy is staying! Not only has he been following them, but he has recording equipment and microphones that captured their affair the night before. He has already sent the evidence to Harge. Carol calls Abby and the two head back home. But at a hotel when Therese falls asleep in Carol's arms, Therese wakes up to find her gone, and Abby there instead. Carol left a note for Therese explaining how they cannot see each other again, even though it is the last thing she wants.

Therese goes back home and develops all the pictures she took of Carol. Meanwhile, Carol spends time with Harge's family. Carol has been going to psychotherapy to cure her homosexuality.

While Dannie helps Therese paint her apartment, he notices all the pictures of Carol and how her photography has turned from landscape to people. He encourages her to put a portfolio together for *The New York Times*. Richard brings Therese a box of her things and tells her that she is different now and he can't forgive her for leaving him and not loving him back. Therese ultimately gets a job at *The Times* hauling developer around all day.

We jump forward to 1953 again where Genevieve writes her address on Therese's hand. Rewind to earlier that day. Therese heads to work and her change is noticeable. She is more elegant. More grown up and mature. Carol spots Therese from the taxi she is taking to the law offices where she meets with Harge, his lawyer, JERRY RIX and Fred. She says that she wants her daughter but she also wanted what happened with

Therese. Carol says she wants Harge to have permanent custody. She doesn't want to mess her daughter's life up, but she wants regular visitation.

Carol writes a letter to Therese but when she receives it, she throws it in a desk drawer. They meet at the Ritz Tower hotel where Carol tells Therese that she is going to be working at a furniture store and moving into a new apartment. She invites Therese to move in with her, but she declines. Then, she invites her to dinner. Just as Carol tells Therese that she loves her, the storylines catch up to one another. Jack arrives and whisks Therese away to Phil's party. Therese leaves the party and walks down the street. She sees Genevieve making out with a woman which prompts her to go meet Carol at the restaurant.

COMMENTS:

This is a great story of forbidden love. Putting a lesbian love story against the backdrop of the 50s, sets that tone right away. In many well-structured, dynamic scenes, it is clear what these women long for and what they are dissatisfied with within their lives. In small scenes just of Therese staring at elderly couples walking lovingly together or Therese's lack of enthusiasm about Richard's European vacation indicates what her want is: to be in love and the audience discovers that alongside Therese. Information isn't given all at once creating an artful use of tension. One example of information being parsed out throughout the script is the mystery of what could be on the telegraph that Carol receives at the hotel. The writer has delivered a well-structured and dynamic story full of intricate scenes that are simple on the surface with so much going on beneath.

Structurally, the midpoint functions the best. It's a great reversal of Therese and Carol finally making love for the first time—the tension that has been holding us through until this point. And then it all comes crashing down the next morning with the realization of Tommy's subterfuge.

In terms of character arcs, Therese's is beautifully articulated. Her status quo in the beginning of the movie is someone who is shy and doesn't really know how to take charge of her life, and the entrance of Carol changes her. Richard even comments on it. She is more mature now. Carol's elegance has rubbed off on her. She has pursued a job at the New York Times. Her arc is very clear, and she is the one who goes through the most change, making it obvious that Therese is the primary protagonist. However, given the script's namesake, Carol lacks in such depth. Her major character beats are brushed over and unarticulated. In the beginning she is an older woman, elusive and semi-hiding who she is from her husband. When her major changes come, like her time at psychotherapy and deciding to give up full custody, these are brushed over in very quick dialogue. One could miss the whole beat of psychotherapy. By the end, she chooses to be happy with the woman she loves, but the beats of her getting to this point are missing.

In regard to format, although the action lines and dialogue of this script are extremely beautiful and grammatically correct, the action lines are THICK. Often times, a Reader has to go back and re-read because the physicality of the scene gets lost within a dense action line. If the length of the action lines is divided up and certain prose-like language that can't be see on the screen is eliminated, it might make for a faster read.

Finally, a major inconsistency that sparks confusion is Therese's initial denial to live with Carol in the third act. After the road trip, Therese shows no signs of bitterness towards Carol. Instead, her apartment is full of pictures of her. So, it doesn't really line up for Therese to decline this offer at first. It doesn't seem motivated. It's understandable that it makes the ending more dramatic to see Therese decide to meet Carol for dinner, but this needs to be set up.

Overall, this is a very moving and emotional love story.

Concept/Originality: EXCELLENT/**GOOD**/FAIR/POOR

Characters: EXCELLENT/**GOOD**/FAIR/POOR

Dialogue: **EXCELLENT**/GOOD/FAIR/POOR

Structure: EXCELLENT/**GOOD**/FAIR/POOR

Format: EXCELLENT/GOOD/**FAIR**/POOR

Script: **RECOMMEND**/CONSIDER/WEAK CONSIDER/PASS

Do you trust the Reader? Do you think you can sell this? Do you see potential? Was it clear? Did you understand the jumping in time? Would you read the script?

Now try this:

You're a network executive for a platform with a well-defined brand. You might even choose a network before reading this. Some examples could be ABC, HBO, FX, AMC, Showtime, or STARZ. Questions you need to answer: Is this a good fit? Can it make money? Is the coverage clear? Do you understand the story? Do you understand the strengths, weaknesses, and potential? Here we go:

BIG TIMEY NETWORK COVERAGE

TITLE: THE BOYS

WRITER: Eric Kripke

FORM: One-hour teleplay

PAGES: 56

SUB BY: XX

SUB TO: XX

ELEMENTS: XX

READER: XX

LOGLINE:

After his girlfriend is murdered by a superhero, Hughie, tech-savvy and naïve, joins forces with Butcher, no-nonsense with a hatred for superheroes, to get revenge.

SYNOPSIS:

HUGHIE, 20s, walks with his girlfriend, ROBIN, 20s, after a shift at an electronics store. As they talk about moving in together, Robin steps off the curb and is obliterated by A-TRAIN, a super-speed superhero, who runs right through her.

STARLIGHT, 20s, nervously auditions for a spot in The Seven, a group of superheroes sponsored by Vought Industries. She shows off her powers and talks about how she wants to save the world.

A VOUGHT LAWYER offers Hughie a large sum of money if he signs an NDA about the Robin incident, but he refuses. BILLY BUTCHER, 40, claiming to be an FBI agent, tells Hughie that he can help get revenge on A-Train. He takes Hughie to a secret superhero-only club, where superheroes are doing all kinds of illegal things. Butcher shows Hughie security footage of A-Train joking about killing Robin.

Starlight is a fan favorite at Vought and goes to thank THE DEEP, a superhero who can speak to fish, for his warm welcome but walks in on him injecting himself with a drug. He chokes her and threatens to kill her if she says anything about what she saw.

JULIA STILLWELL, 40s, Vought's Vice President of Hero Management, tries to sell a superhero to the MAYOR OF BALTIMORE, 50, as his city is experiencing an increase in crime. Remarking that the price is too high, he blackmails Stillwell about a mysterious Compound-V substance.

Butcher tries to convince Hughie to plant a bug inside of Vought by demanding a face-to-face apology with A-Train before signing the NDA but Hughie refuses, scared. Starlight tries to tell HER MOM what happened with The Deep, but her mom is too excited about her becoming a part of The Seven to listen. Hughie and Starlight coincidentally meet on a park bench. They strike up a conversation and find someone who will listen in each other, giving them both the courage to do what they need to do.

Hughie agrees to Butcher's plan and, inside Seven Tower, excuses himself to use the restroom, where he tries to remove the bug from his phone. He drops it as Starlight enters, but she doesn't notice. Hughie successfully plants it underneath a table in the boardroom. However, as he leaves, we see TRANSLUCENT, an invisible superhero, materialize in the bathroom: he's seen the whole thing.

Butcher drops Hughie off at the electronics store, claiming he doesn't need him any longer. Hughie, disappointed, is attacked by Translucent, who followed him back. Butcher saves Hughie and they knock Translucent out, escaping with him.

HOMELANDER, the leader of the Seven, lasers down the airplane of the Mayor of Baltimore.

COMMENTS:

THE BOYS is refreshing, in both relevance and originality, and has the potential to become a popular culture success. In the age of superhero movies, THE BOYS asks the question, "What would superheroes *really* be like?" Instead of Superman, we get Homelander, a psychopath with Superman's powers. Protected by Vought Industries, superheroes are allowed a free pass... in the name of the "greater good." This concept alone is worth expanding upon.

As for the characters, Billy Butcher is the most compelling. This interest comes from his unique and darkly humorous voice and the mystery surrounding his motivations. Hughie and Starlight are passable characters, but they fail to have equally resonant voices. Hughie has a complete character arc, as he gains the courage to fight for what he believes in, but he lacks an engaging personality. Starlight's arc is weaker still. She gains the courage to stand up for herself after being assaulted by The Deep, but we never see her act upon this, which is a missed opportunity. All in all, dramatically, the characters are lackluster; however, the situations they're placed in cover for this weakness.

The real appeal of THE BOYS comes from its setting. This setting is well written, with a level of detail that makes it believable. It drives the story forward, as we want to know what these superheroes are up to in this world. The epitome of this is when Hughie and Butcher enter the Old Money Building, which is a secret superhero-only club, full of debaucherous superheroes. If anything, these moments should be expanded upon.

The plot, like the setting, covers up the weak spots of the characters. Almost every plot point has a satisfying setup and payoff. For example, Hughie watches Translucent, an invisible superhero, on *Ellen* as he talks about how his skin is highly conductive. In the end, Hughie stops Translucent by electrocuting him. These payoffs are effective in establishing an authorial trust, so that, when other setups are not resolved, we trust that they will have a satisfying solution in the coming episodes.

Most importantly, THE BOYS is fun — from the absurdity of Butcher's dialogue to the unabashed graphic portrayal of what superheroes do in their free time: sex, drugs, and rock and roll. In this way, it has the aesthetic of an HBO drama with the subject matter of a Hollywood blockbuster.

In conclusion, THE BOYS is fun, action-packed, and guaranteed to be marketable. While the characters lack some depth, this can be resolved with a character pass, and the intriguing world and satisfying plot more than make up for these grievances.

PROJECT: RECOMMEND

WRITER: RECOMMEND

Remember, most of these projects got made, and so the coverage concludes with a recommend. But do you agree? And how do you see this as a network exec? Also, since the samples in this section aren't going to writers, the Reader can write "they lack some depth" and other comments that might feel a bit harsh if sent to a writer.

And finally:

Here's another TV pilot that's pretty well known. Imagine you are a Netflix exec, and this came across your desk:

THE BIGGEST NETWORK EVER COVERAGE

TITLE: *Montauk* (Later: *Stranger Things*)

WRITERS: Duffer Brothers

FORM: One Hour TV Pilot

PAGES: 65

LOGLINE: A 12-year-old boy goes missing in Montauk 1980's, (a town known for its secret military base once used in the Cold War). And now, his single working mother, an alcoholic police chief, and his three best friends must face the horrors of supernatural forces in order to get him back.

SYNOPSIS: A military base, Camp Hero, explodes, and dozens of scientists inside the laboratory are seen graphically dead. Nearby is the suburban town where MIKE (12) plays the classic 1980s game of *Dungeons and Dragons* with his friends, DUSTIN (12), LUCAS (12), and WILL (12) at his house. At night, they get ready to leave, riding their bikes. Will lives the farthest, and bikes in an empty forest road alone, near Camp Hero.

After encountering A TALL DARK FIGURE on the road, Will turns his bike around but loses control which makes him fall into the forest. He then hears an eerie, guttural sound and spurts home, abandoning his crushed bike. When arriving, nobody is home besides his dog, and the mysterious figure later arrives. Will, terrified, runs to the shed behind his house, where he finds an old rifle on the wall. He then hears thuds against shed doors and the same guttural sound from the forest. It enters inside, but Will does not fire- he is paralyzed with fear. High-pitched, shrieking sounds fill the shed, and it makes the single hanging light bulb glow brighter increasingly. But then, the shrieking sound ends, and the light bulb is back to its normal wattage. The shed is found empty. Will has vanished.

When HOPPER (40s), the police chief, enters work late and hungover like usual, he finds Will's mom, JOYCE (late 30s) waiting impatiently for him. Hopper calms Joyce's worries and takes in her request about finding her son. Meanwhile, at CampHero, THREE AGENTS (ages NA) are at the exploded laboratory searching for answers and we learn that ELEVEN (10), an unknown girl or creature, has survived and escaped. She runs out of the woods and sneaks inside a nearby restaurant — in her bloody hospital gown, shaved buzzed hair, and bare feet. Eleven gets caught, but shortly befriends the restaurant owner, BENNY (40s), and his dog.

Meanwhile, the boys are at school when they get called up to the principal's office to be questioned by Hopper. Once he finally gets the information on Will's most recent whereabouts, he warns the boys very sternly to not search for Will by themselves, which of course, they don't take seriously.

Back at the grill, Benny feeds Eleven, who devours the fish with her bare hands. She doesn't seem to know how to communicate as well, which leads to Benny believing that she is an abused child runaway so he calls the social service number. He notices a car parked out front and is surprised that the social worker he spoke to came so quickly, but he finds it odd that the voice doesn't match the one from the call. As he opens the door, the LADY shoots him from behind- she's an Agent. The other Agents arrive too and scatter into the restaurant searching for Eleven. When spotted, Eleven bursts a metal door toward an Agent, crashing him into the ground — revealing her supernatural powers. When she spots Benny's dead body and the dog's blood on the floor, she cries and runs off once again.

Hopper is out with his team in the forest where Will was last seen and finds Will's crushed bike. He concludes that Will must have been running from something. He stops by Will's house, where Joyce is distraught, worried sick to the point of paranoia. As he looks around the house, he finds the shed outside. In front is Will's dog, whimpering near it, which gives Hopper the notion that something must have happened near the shed.

When picking up the dropped rifle on the ground, the same guttural sound begins again. He thinks it's the dog at first, but the sound continues to get louder and louder. A beam illuminates an approaching figure, and Hopper reaches for his gun until the voice of his coworker interrupts and the coworker steps into the light. Hopper is too shaken to respond and is bleeding from his ear. He leaves the shed nonchalantly but secretly concerned. The shed is left empty, but the guttural sound is low, growing. The same light bulb flickers again, and the wall of the shed appears to have black mold, throbbing and spreading.

It's night again, and Mike and the boys have decided to meet for their own search party. He gets caught by his sister NANCY (16), also sneaking out to go to a party with her best friend BARBARA (16). At the bonfire party, Nancy runs off with a boy, while Barbara hangs out awkwardly at the beach bonfire. It gets late, and Barbara searches for Nancy but gives up. She goes to her car that is parked on an empty road but it won't start. Then the guttural sound comes back again. Then the car headlights grow brighter, and go back to normal.

Barbara is gone.

Joyce is back home anxiously waiting for any news of Will when her older son, JONATHAN (16) comes back looking disappointed — he blames himself for not checking on Will last night. While comforting one another, the two get a mysterious muffled call, and hear a distant voice that sounds like Will. Before they can speak, the phone line dies.

Barbara stumbles onto the beach again. Her face is pale and blood runs out of her ears and nose — she is desperately looking for help, yet, the beach is empty with no trace of the bonfire. A thick fog grows from the ocean, and with it, the wet guttural sound begin again. She sees a horde of dark figures coming towards her. We then cut to an empty forest road where Mike and the boys search for Will —Mike is the most determined out of the group.

While yelling out for Will, a dark figure rushes from the middle of the road and crashes onto the boys, rolling them down to the woods: it's Eleven. She makes direct eye contact with Mike until they hear a rumbling sound. They both look up to the sky. Joyce and Jonathon do as well, as they look through their windows with tear-stained eyes. Hopper looks up at the sky from his car window. Cut to Camp Hero, then again the night sky above, where the low rumbles from the beginning are heard. But this time it grows louder, and electric blue lights flash behind the clouds. The storm has stopped, and "it's here."

COMMENTS: "Montauk" has many familiar 80's sci-fi story elements, but with a distinctive perspective that grabs the viewer's attention. The eerie tone is well established throughout the plot, while capturing the 1980's elements as well. The hook in the beginning grabs our attention with the graphic description of a dying scientist with one leg blown apart struggling to leave the burning Camp Hero Site.

The characters don't really have their own unique personalities. They are tropes that we have seen on TV before — the nerdy middle school boys, the single working mother, and the alcoholic-depressive police. Mike, our main protagonist, is also a bit underwritten and generic. His world is set clear, but there is not enough of an emotional element in driving his determination in searching for Will besides the fact that they are good friends

The only unique character in the story is Eleven — she appears to be human yet acts in an alien way, even having supernatural powers. Moreover, she carries the main tension of the whole story, where she reveals humane aspects of emotions, yet she too is an active part of the dark force that is to arrive. Alongside, her character is also the key to finding Will, as well as revealing the immoral acts that the U.S. military have done.

Structurally, the story does well within the six acts, especially going back and forth between different story lines. This could have possibly made the story confusing and a bit hard to follow, but the writers did a great job in webbing the different subplots all together that begin with the eerie guttural sounds. The only plot line that was off-putting is Nancy's story. Her subplot does not deal with the main conflict of Will's disappearance and the "guttural sounds" and rather focuses on her love life. Moreover, the scene of Steve, her boy crush, who is forcing her to have sex, disrupts the flow of the story and breaks the fearful tension that has been built along — it acts as another anticipated tension that the thriller show already has enough of. Additionally, this scene stirs many different controversial issues that can distort the story plot as well. For example, it deals with issues of sexual abuse and the submissive female character set in the 80's. The strongest attribute to Nancy's story line is from her friend, who gets captured by the alien forces.

Overall, the script is a page turner story, with frantic and exciting beats within each act — we never know what is going to happen next. Many elements play in making this a great pilot: the history of Camp Hero that is yet explained, where Will and the new missing girl have disappeared to, and the questionable existence of Eleven. These will all drive an audience to want to know more and thus continue to watch the show.

PROJECT: RECOMMEND

WRITER: RECOMMEND

Stories with multiple characters, factions and events aren't always easy to summarize. Did you follow the synopsis? Ask yourself if you'd buy it, if the coverage is clear, if it seems profitable (back before you knew it would be) and why. You can also review some of these coverage samples with a critical student's eye and see if there's anything you might do differently.

Why This Understanding Will Put You at the Top of Your Game

If Readers understand and feel what their target audience feels before writing coverage, they will stand head and shoulders above the rest of the herd. Rather than memorizing the rules, they will understand *why* those rules are there.

We can all make a difference with our writing. From the scripts we pen to the guidance we give, to the suggestions we make.

Exercises

This might be the most important set of exercises in this book. When applying for a job as a Reader, you'll find that many companies will ask if you have a coverage sample. If you write a sample coverage for a script that's already been made into a movie, prospective employers will easily understand your notes because they're familiar with the project. But could you criticize or even *pass* on a film that's already successful? I advise my students to *consider* or *recommend* any film that is already produced but also give a few comments or notes as well. Nothing is perfect and your bosses don't want to think that you aren't discerning.

You can also get practice, experience, and do a favor for someone, by finding an unproduced script and write a sample coverage on that. Believe me, you, your friends, your dentist's cousin, Uber drivers — they've all written screenplays and might appreciate getting notes for free.

Here are two exercises that will leave you with two samples to show to prospective employers:

1. Write one practice coverage on a script that was produced, like the *Mad Men* pilot or *Black Panther*.

2. Write one coverage sample on an unknown script that a friend wrote. Potential employers will see that you can effectively convey an unknown story and assess its strengths, weaknesses, potential, and marketability.

19

Giving Verbal Notes

Be Nice, They Know What You Look Like

I'd say about 80% of script notes are written, but there are times when we need to give notes verbally. This means that a Reader must face the writer or their boss and verbally articulate notes, rather than in a document (although they usually need to have one as well).

Which Situations Call for This?

When might these verbal notes happen? At a party? Mostly on Wednesdays? Or in those elevators they keep telling writers they may one day pitch in?

It's simple:

- **Writing instructors** often deliver their notes verbally during class. The students then frantically write them down, record them, or silently disagree and pretend to write them down.

- **Writers in a writing class or writers' group** give each other notes. This is similar to receiving notes from an instructor, except these verbal notes may come from multiple people, often at the same time, which may make the writer feel ganged up on. In order to make verbal notes from a group more effective, I recommend that writer's groups have an established order or set of rules regarding how verbal notes are delivered. Ideally, a writers' group will have strong codes for when to give notes, how to give notes, and how to offer solutions to problems rather than simply point them out.

- **Sometimes, a Reader is asked to give verbal notes to a writer** along with, or instead of, written coverage. This usually happens when working for a coverage service, competition, or private consultation. Some services offer a combination of written notes followed by a consult (via Skype, Zoom, or by phone). I believe it's better to first provide written notes and then use the verbal consult for clarification and follow up questions. This is a better use of the writer's time and allows the Reader to delve deeper.
- **Readers may also give verbal notes when working for an agent or exec.** I also usually include written coverage as well. And again, usually I give verbal notes *after* delivering written coverage, so we can focus on any questions and clarifications.

Verbal Notes for Agents and Execs

Sometimes it's faster for an agent or exec to hear notes verbally. Or they might be lazy. What's more common is for new interns and assistants to pitch or discuss projects they've read as part of their training. Some companies hold weekly meetings where they do this.

I once had to "pitch projects" in a development job interview. I don't mean like how a writer pitches their project to sell it — I mean I was asked to convey my notes verbally. I had to tell them the story, what worked, what didn't, and then give my recommendation. Executives give this same type of verbal pitch/coverage at their company's internal meetings and to their higher-ups. So, Readers who want to climb the corporate ladder need to learn this skill.

Pros and Cons of Verbal Notes

When a Reader writes coverage that is sent to a writer, what are the advantages and disadvantages compared to giving verbal notes?

Written Notes

Pros
- The Reader can take time to formulate opinions.
- The Reader's facial expressions do not matter.

- The Reader and writer will likely never meet.
- The writer will have written documentation of your notes.
- The task of covering a script is done, over, and filed in a database.

Cons

- We can't always satisfactorily explain what we mean.
- Written notes are open to interpretation by the writer.
- And for the executive, written notes are impersonal and make the Reader just one of many turning in a report.

Verbal Notes

Pros

- You can have a conversation with the writer and if they don't understand something, you can immediately clarify it.
- You can get to know the writer and see if you're helping them.
- You can ask what the writer's intention was for the script, scene, character, etc.
- When giving notes verbally to an executive, you're in the game! They hear your opinion.

Cons

- You might be nervous and think of this as some sort of performance.
- You must look and sound professional. Facial expression and tone of voice matter. It can be hard to hide if you dislike something or are nervous.
- You face the writer directly, which can be hard. If they are sensitive or defensive, you'll have to deal with it.
- And for the executive, there's no hiding behind a report.

I've done all the above. And so far, every time I have a verbal or online consultation with a writer I'm nervous, and yet every time, it goes well! My favorite thing is when I see that they got a great new idea and are excited to implement it. Then I can say "Go. Get off this call and write it while it's fresh!" And they do.

Fake It 'Til You Make It

It's scary to give verbal notes to an executive you want to impress. Whether for a writer or a boss, how do you maintain professionalism and confidence and not turn into a human sprinkler of sweat and drool? Remember one thing: it's not about you.

If a writer hired you, they know you have some sort of caché. At the very least, since you didn't write the script they know you'll be able to help them with blind spots.

When I meet or talk to writers, I ask them about themselves and what led them to write their script. Was it based on something true? Do they have a knowledge or passion for some aspect of it? And we connect. I then forget about me (and this gets easier the more one does this) and focus on the script, the writer's needs, and how to help both. I also take in what type of person they are to see if I can ease their nervousness with humor, assure them of the script's strengths, and so on. I focus and lose myself in the job as I make sure they understand what I'm saying about *their* project.

When Writers Want You to Solve Their Issues

Executives and agents might ask for possible solutions to problems that are described in verbal notes. They may even take your suggestions and relay them to the writers. Remember, your job is to make the executive's job easier. Impress and make them look good and they will hopefully remember.

If you find yourself being asked directly by an exec to give feedback, you can state your opinions but you must be sure to read the boss and/or the room (and maybe do some homework ahead of time) so that you know what the exec is looking for.

With a writer, be more careful about providing solutions. I've worked with writers who ask, "What would you do?" Tiny fixes may be okay to suggest, and I always try to find the easiest solution so they don't break all the bones in their script and start from scratch. But for big decisions, I try to guide them to their own answers.

Both writers and students should be encouraged to experiment and explore, to try things, and then more things. Often after they test something out only to end up eliminating it, they then find something even better.

Help them trust their voice. Don't speak for them.

Exercises

1. Imagine you read a writer's early draft of a script after being hired to give them verbal notes. You didn't like it and felt that the characters had no arcs, the stakes were low, the protagonist was passive, and the plot was all over the place. How would you prepare for this verbal, one-hour meeting? How might you organize and phrase your critique in a way that won't overwhelm, dissuade, or panic this new writer? Consider writing

out bullet points of the main points you will make, knowing of course, that if you knew the specifics of the script, you could offer some concrete suggestions. List what you would go over and how you might approach each topic.

2. Same new and flawed script as in the above example. This time however, you already sent a writer a 3- to 5-page written coverage before the verbal consultation.

    A.   Before starting, how do you prepare so you are emotionally and psychologically ready to do this? Think of your face, tone, posture, and attitude.

    B.   You see the writer, they have your notes, and they seem quite nervous. What might you open up with to put them at ease? Do you make small talk? Compliment them?

    C.   What if they say, "I didn't agree with your notes. I don't think you got what I was trying to do at all." What would be your response? Remember, they can see you.

    D.   You're back on track and discussing how the protagonist has very low stakes for driving to Montana on a road trip. They sigh, agree and then ask, "What should I do?" What do you say?

3. You work for an agent who asks you to pitch them the project you just covered for them. Remember that they haven't read the script.

    A.   How will you prepare to give verbal notes? (Yes, you can bring documents or a laptop/tablet.) What are some steps you might take for the presentation? And no, it doesn't have to be a PowerPoint extravaganza with visuals. You are relaying the story and your comments.

    B.   What if you have a similar, better script and the agent asks, "What you would do?" You absolutely want them to chuck this one and buy yours! Write down some possible actions and answers you could take, ranging from the most-humble, non-writing servant to the most self-promoting, super-writer. What do you think is appropriate?

    C.   You read for an agent that never reads their client's scripts, they just want to sell them. They ask you to relay the details of the script so they can sound like they read it themselves. How might that affect your notes? And for a bonus question, what if you're then in the room with them when they meet with their client who wrote the script and the agent gets a few things wrong? What are some possible actions you could take, if any? Write down a few options based on the people and situation involved.

20

For the Writer

Now That You Understand the Coverage
Process, How Can You Make It Work for You?

Whether reading becomes a side job, a main job, or funds a nice nose job, writers learn a lot from reading and critiquing other scripts. Some people picked up this book because they really want to become a Reader, but some might just want to know how to appease them. Throughout the book, I hope that writers gained valuable insight into what Readers are looking for. In this chapter, I'm going to shift focus to *the writer* and share insider tips specifically for them that I learned from years of experience as both a Reader and a development executive.

Competitions

Screenwriting competitions are great for all writers, especially new writers, writers who don't have an agent, or writers who live outside of Los Angeles (although Zoom makes that easier now). Winners get some money, validation, and on a few rare occasions, the script gets made and their career gets launched.

If a script places (quarterfinalist, semifinalist, finalist) but does not win a screenplay competition, there are still many opportunities available. First, there's the validation that it beat out many others, so it must be good. Second, many competitions announce and promote their finalists to potential buyers, sellers, and reps. Third, writers who place in a competition often still get some financial compensation. Finally, since many competitions are judged by industry professionals, who knows? One of them may like a script and contact the writer outside of the competition.

When I was hired to read for one of the top agencies, my first assignment was to read all the Nicholl Fellowship semifinalists. Semifinalists! That means that even as a semifinalist, a writer still benefits. Imagine a writer being bummed out they didn't win a competition, and then out of nowhere they get a call from a top agency. It can happen!

My standard advice to all quarter-, semi-, and regular finalists is to contact execs and reps and tell them they were a finalist in *Big Ol' Screenplay Competition.* There are countless reasons why a certain script wins but it still takes talent to make it to the semi-finals, and execs know this.

I also advise writers to contact people in the film and TV industry and promote themselves once they know they're a semi-finalist or finalist *before the winner is announced.* Their script could still win, so execs will know they advanced and may want to read the script before it wins and everyone else comes after it.

The bottom line is: winning isn't everything. There's a lot to be gained by entering and placing in competitions.

What Are Competitions Looking For?

Different competitions look for different things, although all will say that they want great stories and writing. The Nicholl usually wants depth, and its winning scripts are rarely comedies. Slamdance wants independent films, and there are also competitions aimed at Black, LGBTQ+, Latinx stories, and others. If there's a specific focus, it's usually stated in the guidelines, so writers must do their homework before paying the entry fee.

But what don't they tell us?

A Behind-the-Scenes Look at Judging

There are forces beyond a writer's control. Make no mistake, to become a finalist or semifinalist a writer has to have talent, (and more than one Reader who likes their script) but when it comes to the winner…? Sometimes a competition wants to make a statement with the winning script. They want it to be current, timely, political, contain social justice issues, or fulfill some other agenda. I've heard that some want to showcase a script that they think *could be made* so they can say that they aided in its discovery. Or sometimes if the top five scripts are all in the same genre, they might swap one of them out for another genre to widen the spectrum.

I've seen competitions where some scripts get a high score in one category and a lower score in another but the judges agreed to go for something that got pretty good/average marks across the board. For example, a script might have received a 10 on story and a 5 on structure but they went with something that got solid 7's.

My point is: if a writer doesn't win, they'll never know why. If they win one competition and not others, they won't know why. If a writer places, it means they're good but they'll never know why they didn't win. If a writer gets feedback with their submission, they might know what each Reader thought, but they should take it with a grain of salt. If one Reader loved it and another hated it, that doesn't mean a writer should do a total rewrite.

To have the best chance, I recommend adhering to the rules and consider what makes a Reader happy: a well written, emotionally engaging, clear, active, well structured, character-driven story — one that's rich, vivid, tells just enough, uses wonderful language, and has sharp dialogue and descriptions.

Of course all scripts should also have a great title, be under 120 pages, have correct formatting, hook the Reader from the start, be familiar yet different, and have a unique voice and POV.

Finding Representation

Writers usually enter a competition to get noticed but they submit their scripts to an agent to get themselves and/or their project represented. What are agents and managers looking for? Beyond just liking a script these people may represent the writer as a client. While agents usually have more clout, take a mandated 10%, and often have more clients and less personal touch than managers, they both want *career longevity*. Reps want a client whose writing they can consistently sell, and many want their jobs to be easy. Therefore, they want a great script *and* a wonderful client, so they can market both.

This is why a manager can be a good option. They usually take a 15% cut, have fewer clients, give more of a personal touch, may be more open to finding and cultivating new writers, and sometimes want to attach themselves as a producer.

Both agents and managers want to know if they can make money off of the writer. And if they're not sure yet the project is killer, they may not sign someone as a client but offer instead to work on that specific project.

Some represent directors or actors and are looking at a script to see if it's a good fit. Writers submitting to an agent with a big client should research and see what that client is seeking for their next role. Do they want that Oscar-bait part? To bust out of a stereotype or typecasting? To act in something their grandkids would like?

Agents and managers receive countless scripts, so writers must make theirs stand out. Make the script the best it can be. Remember that unlike with a competition, a script can be rewritten, so while the script doesn't have to be perfect, a writer must still make it as good as possible, especially for those reps (mostly agents) who want to sell, not develop, a project or writer.

What Are Development Execs Looking For?

Like agents and managers, a development exec wants to find great scripts. However, they usually are looking to buy for a network, studio, or production company. Writers shouldn't just submit their work to an exec blindly, they need to do their homework, check out a company's websites, and read interviews with key executives — where they often state their vision very clearly.

Take a look at Morgan Freeman's company, Revelations Pictures' mission statement:

> "To 'reveal truth,' drives company to produce thought-provoking entertainment with artistic integrity and "soul."

If they're a company that develops and sells projects to someone else, they'll work with a writer and take it out to potential buyers. For example, perhaps a writer gets a production company such as Jennifer Lopez' Nuyorican Productions to take their script to Netflix, where they have a deal. Then Nuyorican may work with the writer to further develop the script before they take it to Netflix. Many writers are best served by getting their projects to production companies (often called *pods*), since they have names, track records and deals, and once attached to the project, can open bigger doors.

A script doesn't have to be perfect for a company to be interested — they'll have notes and work with the writer to develop it further. In some cases, they may bring on another writer (or writers) to rewrite it. However, execs want to see the talent, potential and marketability on the page.

Reasons execs may say no:

- Not a great script.
- Not a great writer.
- Not a great Reader (they couldn't see the script's potential).
- The script seems unprofessional.

- Not what they're looking for.
- They already have something similar.
- The market doesn't want this right now.

Remember, at every level of the business there are both masters of the craft and people who "lucked their way up." A writer may submit to subpar Readers or subpar execs. They need to make their scripts as tight and professional as they can and when all the heavy lifting is done, edit for errors and consider how to make it an even better reading experience.

Exercises

1. Research at least three different screenwriting competitions. Some examples are Slamdance, The Sundance Lab, Scriptapalooza, Script Pipeline, Final Draft, PAGE, Coverage Ink, and the Nicholl Fellowship. For TV there are some diversity-focused contests such as NBC Writers on the Verge, the Warner Bros. and Disney Fellowships. *Coverfly* often lists quite a few. See which ones tell you what they're looking for, if they have a specific bent, and then look at the titles and loglines of the winners and semifinalists. Do you see consistency? Is there a pattern?

2. Read a very successful script that is known for its writing. Some examples are scripts that won best writing Oscars and Emmys, or films and TV shows that got excellent reviews or word of mouth for writing. For example, many TV writers love *The Wire* and *Breaking Bad*. Or look at a show that ran for a long time and got critical acclaim, such as *Seinfeld*. The point is to read something known for its craft. Ask yourself: "What can I apply to my own writing?" Readers, even if you're not a writer, you should try this as well. It will help you find a standard to hold future scripts to.

3. Find an unproduced script, a produced script that got critically panned, a TV pilot that never got made into a series or a show that was cancelled right away. Now take the scripts apart to learn what doesn't work.

21

The Coverage Business

Get Ready to Work!

Who Uses Readers?

Let's stop for a moment and take a little quiz. Everyone should be able to answer this by now, and if not… *they weren't paying attention.*

So, this quiz is the hardest one ever made. Here it is:

Who uses Readers?

- A   Agents.
- B   Production companies.
- C   Networks.
- D   Script Services.
- E   Screenplay Competitions.
- F   Studios.
- G   Writers hire them personally.
- H   Little kids who want a bedtime story.
- I   All of the above.

The answer is *I*. And for those looking for the job of answer *H*, I wish them well in having a child with a lovely, little children's book library and I've got little else to tell them.

Agents and execs want Readers to make their job easy. So, when they interview a potential hire or look at their resume/CV, they want to see that they have experience with writing or coverage and are professional. If they're seeking an intern, they know they'll have to train them so it's good for an applicant to present themselves as a quick learner. It's always good to show experience, so be sure to do the exercises in this book in order to have some good samples when you're done.

If an applicant placed or won competitions, is repped by an agent or manager, or can think of anything else that shows they know screenwriting, be up-front with that information. The same goes for other kinds of writing. I've taught coverage classes to English professors, ex-journalists, and lawyers who knew how to write, critique, and present an opinion. That all can count as experience and should be included in one's resume and cover letter.

Perhaps a potential hire has worked in the industry in another area. I had a client who was a film editor. They knew movies, the business, and how to make something tighter and better. People can use life experiences to show that they understand movies, writing, and how to give notes. They should focus on the fact that they already know how to assess writing, they can vet the best, weed out the worst, help writers, and understand needs of the company or brand.

If you are applying for a job as an assistant, know that many companies hire people who can take calls, understand the business, know social media, and have whatever other skills assistants need to have. So being able to write coverage is a definite plus.

It's a similar situation when applying to competitions and coverage services. These companies make money based on their reputations, so they want strong Readers. A literary agent's assistant may have to pick up their wife when she's waiting for her car to be fixed (personal experience here) *and* read scripts. But competitions and coverage services only want to know one thing: Does an applicant know how to rate scripts and write coverage?

How to Get a Gig

After making your CV or resume all spiffy, I suggest the following: If you has never written coverage, you should create a sample. Prospective Readers can make their own template or adapt those I've provided in Chapter 2 and the appendix at the end of the book.

Again, if you do the exercises in this book, you'll have multiple samples to show. I recommend having at least two samples: one of an unknown/unproduced work and one of a known/produced work. One of those could be a coverage for a writer and the other for an agent or network using the templates I've provided.

Prospective employers will tell an applicant which they want to read. Some may want to read both and some may just be impressed with the range of samples.

Others may administer a "test sample" where they provide a script for the applicant to cover. This will be a script they already know and they may or may not provide a template. (Personally, I would always ask if they have one.) I still recommend having samples ready because it impresses them that a person has them and, the applicant has already done some and will be more prepared for this "test."

Another way to get experience and produce a sample is to get an internship with a competition that asks Readers to work for free. (They understand that starting Readers will do this for the experience.)

As for where to look for work, there are many sites and job boards such as *Entertainmentcareers.net*, *Coverfly*, and others. *LinkedIn* can help and I've even seen listings on *Craigslist*. Other Readers, interns, and assistants find out about jobs too, so people who want to become Readers should figure out who they know. They can also cold call companies and find out if they're hiring.

Studio executives have a lot to do and a lot of people to deal with. Be personable but the best way to stand out might be to not stand out. Readers often must be quiet and just do their job. Therefore, prospective hires should make their cover letters or inquiries short, succinct, and catchy. Since Readers are hired to make their boss' job easier, an applicant should show they can do that by not taking up any extra time or space in the application process.

Compensation

To gain experience, there are a lot of opportunities for Readers to work for free. Whether it's a friend asking someone to read their script, or a festival that asks ex-winners and alumni to judge for free as a way to "give back," don't be surprised to find a lot of non-paid Reading work.

I sometimes do free consults or reads for ex-students, friends, and other writers. Writers should keep note of the peers whose opinions they respect, because we all need another pair of eyes. However, they must establish boundaries. Readers must learn when to say "no" or "not yet."

The other type of free work is of course working as an intern. Often interns work for college credit, a resume credit, experience, training, and hopefully to network at or even get hired by a company.

Here's something to consider (Table 21.1) for those interested in applying for a job as a literary assistant or an assistant to any agent, manager, development department, etc. As of 2021:

Literary Agent Assistant Salary in Los Angeles, CA

	Annual Salary	Monthly Pay
Top Earners	$94,763	$7,896
75th Percentile	$52,940	$4,411
Average	$47,446	$3,953
25th Percentile	$30,705	$2,558

Table 21.1

Salary ranges for Literary Assistants.

In most cases, when a Reader freelances for companies, competitions, and services there's a range of pay but it isn't very high. For most people, Reading is usually a supplemental career.

Big companies and agencies often pay more, but not always. A while ago, a top agency paid $50/script and compensated even more for *rushes* (a very quick turnaround, such as 1-3 days) or for longer scripts. Nowadays many companies pay $100 and more. One cable network pays $100/script and added $50 bonuses for rushes and anything over 120 pages. They paid even more for long books. It's the luck of the draw.

For example: One agency paid $40-$45 and wanted over seven pages of coverage and a lot of extra details (work). They would also assign coverage on a Friday afternoon and ask for them to be done by Monday, calling it a weekend read but not a rush. By contrast, the cable network that paid $100 was simple, they gave Readers about a week or so to create the coverage and it only needed to be 3-4 pages long.

Each company is different. Readers must figure out if this is just side work, if connections are more important, if they're doing this to learn how to be a better writer, etc. A Reader might take less money and do more work reading at a big company because they hope to make connections and submit their own writing to them one day.

Competitions can start as low as $20-25 for a quick score or rating and paragraph (which, depending on how quickly one reads could average to $20-25/hour). Some will ask for 2-4 pages of coverage as well and pay about $40-$60, with many paying more for scripts over 120 pages, rushes, and semi-rushes.

Many coverage services will pay more than a competition does and ask for more work. They charge writers more because their focus is on guidance and critique. Some pay $60-$80 and ask for around 5-8 pages of notes. Depending on how much of a perfectionist a Reader is, the speed at which they read and make notes, and how enjoyable the script is, it could take a short or a long time. If a Reader finds themself spending six hours on coverage, this doesn't work out too well as an hourly rate.

Private coverage is the wild west. People can charge a little or a lot. I know a screenwriting professor that charged $10,000 for a consult many years ago and I always wondered why the writer didn't just take that money and make a cheap film. I've worked for companies that paid $100 for me to give a consult, and then discovered that they charged a lot more and kept a huge percentage. The same occurred with a one-month mentorship for a writer — the company's percentage was huge.

The workload varies and the pay varies. I've seen the pay scale rise over time, and hopefully it will continue to do so. And the more a Reader does, the better they become, the better their resume looks, and the more they can charge.

Exercises

1. Make a resumé or CV for Reader jobs. Include anything pertinent, such as reading, writing, critiquing, coaching, English or journalism degrees, competitions entered, workshops, or training.

2. Write a succinct, catchy, and professional cover letter to use. Make it personal to a company's brand or interests.

3. Since in previous exercises you created sample coverage, get them ready and proofread them.

4. Earlier, you researched possible sites for competitions and/or companies you want to work for. Research more, and when the above materials are ready, apply. Scour industry job boards, competitions, and coverage services. Check *Coverfly* for a list of reading job opportunities. Check places like the Austin Film Festival screenplay competition, that often use unpaid writers who want to get a foot in the door and a resumé credit in return for their work. Perhaps find a non-college internship if you aren't in college. Look at other places that utilize Readers and offer coverage services. Make a list of anyone in the entertainment industry and ask if they know of opportunities.

22

Final Thoughts

Tricks I Can Pass On

When I was five, I read this *Sesame Street* book called *The Monster at The End of This Book: Starring Lovable, Furry Old Grover.* In it, Grover kept saying not to keep turning pages because there was a monster at the end of the book. I won't spoil the ending (it's a great twist), but I feel the same way. I want my readers to stop turning pages because when they get to the end, we'll have to say goodbye.

And I don't want to.

But a good teacher guides and then must let their little birds leave the nest.

So, some last-minute comments to both Readers and writers alike.

Do Sweat the Small Stuff

Well, don't sweat. We should relax and nurture ourselves. But remember, the small things can mean a lot. And I don't just mean sweet gestures to the people we love, I mean those small details:

Formatting, grammar, spelling, using the active voice, keeping it concise — both in our screenplays and coverage—will all ensure our work appears professional and is not discounted.

Readers, ask how each company wants their coverage done, see if there's a template, and ask questions up front — to know the taste of the executive or company and to be able to locate projects that fit it. Remember, our job is to summarize the story for them and let them know how far along it is.

When doing coverage for a writer, guide and encourage them whenever possible but also be clear and concise since they'll read the coverage through their own filters. And with verbal notes, it's important to get out of our heads and be present in the room.

How to Stand Out

In interviews, Readers are often asked what types of movies or TV shows they like. They should research the company they're applying and shouldn't be obvious or kiss their tushy, but perhaps mention one of theirs. Or something like theirs. For example, if we interview with the Hallmark channel and our favorite shows are horror, they better be Christmas horror movies, i.e.: *The Santaman — He knows when you are sleeping…*

Remember for both the cover letter and interview, we're there to make *their* job easier. We'll stand out if our context is: "How can I help?" Applicants should be aware of what *they* can provide. Are they a quick reader or easy to get along with? Perhaps they love a genre that not many do or are psychic and know what will sell next year. What can we bring to their table?

Readers provide a service — to writers and to execs and agents. Speak to that.

If it's a job that gives coverage directly to writers, we should show that we know how they think and feel, how we want to help, guide, and inspire, and that we have a positive attitude. They want their clients to have a great experience. Speak to that.

Cheat Sheets and Time-Saving Skills

Having done this for years, there are notes I find myself giving repeatedly, so I've made a cheat sheet of sorts. I always give personalized individual notes, but a few things can be inserted, adapted, or used as an opening.

For example:

> Parentheses within dialogue must be indented and
> on their own line within the dialogue itself.

Or:

> There are a lot of characters introduced all at once
> and it's hard to keep track. Introduce characters
> gradually and distinctly.

These are issues I come across often and so can copy and paste these along with more specific notes.

Or, since I often find that by the end of Act One the protagonist isn't driving the plot, I can take from my cheat sheet the following:

> By the end of a first act (usually around pages 25-
> 30), the protagonist should begin their pursuit of a
> high stakes goal. At the end of this script's first act...

And add in the specific note: "We're not sure who the protagonist is." "They're still considering their goal." "It's more like a situation than a quest."

I put in a lot of time and effort into coverage, but if it's a note I give often, cheat sheets can help. As a Reader goes along, they can craft their own. As far as how to save time, that varies from person to person. For some coverages, a Reader might read the whole script and write the coverage from memory. Others may read and write their notes simultaneously. Some read sections, such as one act at a time and then write up each act. If you're giving a lot of technical or page-specific comments, you may have to write notes as you go.

Reading is great but it can be sedentary and draining. Try different locations and get up and move around. We have to take care of ourselves. Also, it's good to protect our eyes from blue light if possible.

Apps We Like: *PDF Expert*

PDF Expert is a free app and it's great. I'll read and make notes on the PDF doc on my iPad, write up my main notes, and then go back and add the smaller ones.

Don't Take Things Personally

Working as a Reader especially in a corporate environment, can feel like we're in a factory assembly line: Read, submit, hear nothing, read, submit, hear nothing. Or we sometimes get a note or criticism on something. The former is the nature of the beast — there's little immediate gratification or validation. In time you might be asked for advice or clarification, learn that something you recommended will be made, or something you passed on is made by another company. It's all part of the gig.

As far as receiving criticism from the bosses, take it. Put it into the context of, "Are you making their job easier or not?" This should remove the personal sting. Ask how to be more effective. If your boss gives you a note on your coverage, it's a chance to improve. You didn't fail. Something was missing and now you know how to elevate it.

You'll never meet most of the writers you work with. When you do, you can get validation or criticism. As you start out there will be much to learn and adjust along the way. Rather than becoming despondent or hard on yourself, adopt the mantra, "Correct and continue." How can you improve?

If you get a defensive, negative, or arrogant writer, remember they are sensitive and vulnerable. It's their work on the line. You can explain yourself, give up that point if they don't agree, let go, and move on. You will feel a pang if you hear negative feedback on your feedback. But look at it. Is it true or helpful? Will it improve your skills? If so, then apply their note. If not, thank them and move on.

Remember: *you can't please everyone.*

Truthful, Heartfelt Good Wishes and Encouragement — Because It's What I Believe

And now we come to the monster at the end of the book but, it's a nice monster. An encouraging one. One that breaks the fourth wall and talks to you personally.

It's strange that I have a bit of sadness ending this book, in the same way as when a class ends. I may not know you personally, but like the writers you are and the Readers you'll become, I've opened my thoughts and feelings to you and that gives us a bit of a bond.

I'll wrap up, as you have a wonderful and bright future living your dreams and contributing to the dreams of others.

My writing, reading, and teaching have all been to develop, hone, refine and help people express their visions and voices. When I started out reading, I didn't know I could make a difference, but now I do…

And that has made all the difference.

We all have stories to tell, and I'm honored to help others tell theirs. Reading scripts has exposed me to perspectives, events, stories, and worlds

I never knew, and has let me into the hearts and minds of extraordinary people.

You are one of those people. You can rate scripts, clear stacks from your boss' inbox, make a buck, etc. But if you're lucky you get feedback like this:

> My producing partner, Neto Pimenta, and I, had the pleasure of meeting with Beverly Neufeld in her capacity as a script and film project consultant through Slamdance. We didn't know what to expect at first, but it couldn't have been more helpful and enjoyable. Beverly was punctual, polite, and professional. She analyzed the script with us from several different perspectives, giving us insights which we didn't realize, and significantly aiding us in improving the material. We gained new confidence about the direction we were headed primarily because Beverly's analysis was always positive and it's clear her goal was to make the project the best it can be. She went above and beyond and even gave us a contact to help in our research of the script's source material.
>
> In addition to all this, Neto and I found ourselves genuinely having fun through the entire process. We felt a definite rapport with Beverly. She is genuine, sincere, and funny. We all noted that we would stay in touch and from our end we will continue to apprise her of our developments with this project. I would wholeheartedly recommend Beverly for any script analysis or consultation required.
>
> *Best, Atul Sharma*

I wish you luck, success, fulfillment, fun, joy, and the path to your dreams.

Thank you for being a part of my journey and heart.

Beverly Neufeld

Appendix

In Chapter 2, I provided three examples of coverage templates. Here are three additional examples:

A Different Screenwriting Competition Report

This is an example of a more detailed screenwriting competition report that would be seen by a writer. It lists many topics and categories that readers use.

> **Title:** Insert title
>
> **Form:** Screenplay, teleplay?
>
> **Genre:** What genre is it?
>
> **Setting:** Time and place.
>
> **Budget:** High? Medium? Low?
>
> **Page Count:** How many pages? (Not including the title page.)
>
> Reader's Initials: Add your initials.
>
> **Date:** Month/Day/Year of coverage report.
>
> 1. Logline: Give a one or two sentence logline.
>
> 2. In what ways is the writer successful at achieving his/her goals? This should be roughly three paragraphs on the script's strengths. What works?
>
> 3. In what ways does the screenplay fall short? Roughly three paragraphs on how to improve it. What needs work?
>
> 4. On the contest scorecard, you gave this script a total score of: <u>Add the points you'll give below</u>. Please explain your criteria for your score.
>
> Please rate each category from 1-10 with 10 being the highest.
>
> <u>PREMISE/CONCEPT</u> Score: *Give a score from 1-10.*
>
> *Supply detail of the premise or concept and justify your* score.
>
> <u>PRESENTATION</u> Score: Give a score from 1-10.
>
> *Note details in formatting, grammar, mechanics, and professionalism and justify your score.*
>
> <u>STRUCTURE</u> Score: Give a score from 1-10.
>
> *Explain the structure of the story, hitting the plot points, set-ups and pay-offs, and the tracking of external and internal arcs. Justify your score.*
>
> <u>PLOT</u> Score: *Give a score from 1-10.*

Details about the story, its points, logic, consistency, etc. Justify your score.

PACING Score: *Give a score from 1-10.*

Provide details of repetition, stakes, momentum, if it escalates or starts and stops, etc. Justify your score.

CHARACTERS Score: *Give a score from 1-10.*

Supply details about how distinctive and three-dimensional the characters are, if they evolve, and if they are active or passive. Justify your score.

DIALOGUE Score: *Give a score from 1-10.*

Offer details about subtext or "on-the-nose" dialogue, language that is too technical, voices that sound too similar, and characters who refer to things they might know but we don't. Justify your score.

THEME Score: *Give a score from 1-10.*

Include details about how messages are conveyed, if they're too subtle or too heavy-handed, and if characters have arcs so we learn along with them as they grow and change. Justify your score.

STYLE/TONE Score: *Give a score from 1-10.*

Discuss the writer's style and whether or not it's bold, clear, creative, or original. Is the tone compelling and consistent.? Justify your score.

COMMERCIAL POTENTIAL Score: *Give a score from 1-10.*

Provide details of the marketability of this project. Is it a small independent project or a huge studio film? What will help attract buyers, sellers, and talent? What's there and what's missing? Justify your score.

5. RECOMMEND   CONSIDER   PASS

This is where you rate it by underlining one or using bold font.

6. **How could this writer improve his/her chances of success with this script?** *Don't bring up any new points. This is the conclusion or summation of what you already said. Again, I often break down the steps for a rewrite and leave on an encouraging note.*

Network Coverage Report

This is an example of a template for a network that won't be seen by the
writer.

TITLE: *Insert title.*

WRITER: *Insert the writer's (or writers') name(s).*

FORM: *Screenplay, teleplay, book?*

PAGES: *How many pages? (Not including the title page.)*

SUB BY: *They will inform you if someone submitted it (like an agent or a production company).*

SUB TO: *They will inform you which executive this was submitted to.*

ELEMENTS: *They will inform you if anyone is attached, like an actor, director, etc.*

READER: *Your name.*

LOGLINE: *Give a one or two sentence logline.*

SYNOPSIS: *About three-quarters to one page: This is where, in paragraph form and in third person, you tell the story of the script, hitting the important facts. As with a screenplay, all new characters are introduced in capital letters, with their ages given.*

COMMENTS: *About 1 page:*

Here's where your main notes are given — in essay form. You can refer to page numbers to give examples or for things you "bump up against." Watch your tone and inform the executive about the project's strengths and weaknesses, as well as the project's possible potential and if it is a good match for the network brand. Do not use "I" or "me" and do not address the executive directly.

PROJECT: RECOMMEND/CONSIDER/WEAK CONSIDER/PASS

WRITER: RECOMMEND/CONSIDER/WEAK CONSIDER/PASS

This is where you rate each category by underlining one of the choices or using bold font.

Here, you can state that while this project might not be right for the network, the writer has potential (and may have other work that's a better fit for the network).

My Template for Private Consultations

This one is something I came up with for when I give private consultations — this will be seen by the writer.

Title: *Insert title.*

Author: *Insert the writer's (or writers') name(s).*

Genre: *What genre is it?*

Pages: *How many pages? (Not including the title page.)*

Covered by: *Your name.*

Date: *Month/Day/Year of coverage.*

LOGLINE: Give a one or two sentence logline.

COMMENTS: *Don't write anything on this line. It just delineates that we will now go into comments below:*

Overall: *Here is where I give an overall impression of what works and then what might need work. I usually write two paragraphs here - one for the strengths and one for what might need work.*

Technical: *This is where I mention any formatting, grammar, or mechanical issues. I don't list all typos, as proofreading and editing are different assignments. However, if there are errors, I might end with a statement that there are one or two, a few, or numerous typos.*

ACT ONE: *Here I would begin by providing an overall note on Act One and then give more specific comments. Then I go into detail and cite examples of any and all issues.* Watch your tone, be constructive, don't use "I" or "you", etc.

ACT TWO*: I then do the same for Act Two.*

ACT THREE: *And I do the same for Act Three.*

SUGGESTIONS FOR A REWRITE: *Don't bring up any new points. This is the conclusion or summation of what you already said. I often reassure them that it's not a lot of work and break down the steps for a rewrite. I always end on an encouraging note.*

Glossary

arcs The journey of a character, plot, or relationship throughout a script. Internal arcs are how a character transforms over time, while external arcs are journeys we can see and track.

buyers These are people who can make the decision to buy a script, such as producers, studios, investors, and networks.

cold open Short for *cold opening*, this TV script device comes at the beginning of the show, usually before the opening credits. Cold opens don't have to relate to the rest of the episode's plot and can be a quick mini opening act. A cold open typically features main characters and introduces the show's tone.

coverage A report on a script, usually done by a reader, for a boss or a writer.

development The process of finding, working with, and preparing a project to the point where it's ready to go to casting and pre-production.

development executives People who work on acquiring ideas and scripts, and getting them ready to be cast and made.

elements attached Within script coverage, this means that the script already has someone (like an actor, director, or producer) attached to it.

four quadrants When a film or show can attract audiences of all genders, both above and below a certain age range.

gatekeepers A term for readers to describe that they are the first ones to usually read a script and recommend it to the next level.

genre A stylistic category based on setting, characters, plot, mood, tone, and theme.

high-concept idea A type of artistic work that can be easily pitched with a succinctly stated premise.

inciting incident The event that sets the main character or characters on the journey that will occupy them throughout the narrative. It usually occurs up to or around the 10 page/10 minute mark.

low-concept idea A story that puts focus on the world and characters surrounding the plot, instead of the plot itself.

mark A structural point in a script which the industry usually expects, such as an inciting incident occurring around page 10, the end of Act One occurring around pages 25-30, etc.

marketability The extent to which a film can attract an audience and make a lot of money.

mechanics The non-creative aspects of a screenplay, such as formatting and grammar.

multi-camera scripts A script (usually for TV) intended to be filmed with multiple cameras in front of a live studio audience.

option Contracted permission that gives interested parties exclusive development and shopping rights to a screenplay for a specific amount of time.

pilot The first episode of a TV show.

procedural In TV, a genre of programs in which a problem is introduced, investigated, and solved all within the same episode.

private consultations When a reader or script consultant works for themselves, rather than at a company, script service or competition.

runner Usually a tiny plot line or joke that goes on for the length of a script.

script competition A competition where scripts compete to place and then win a prize. These usually employ readers, involve judges, can also provide coverage for additional payments, and many are seasonal (once a year).

script reader A person hired to read and review a script and then write an analysis and recommend if it should go to the next level or not. Readers can work for film and TV companies, studios, networks, executives, producers, and agents, for script services, competitions or have a private consultation business.

script services Companies that provide coverage and feedback for writers on their scripts. Some are affiliated with competitions, and some aren't

sellers People who try to sell scripts to buyers, mostly agents and managers. Some writers and lawyers also try to sell scripts to buyers.

set-ups and pay-offs Within a script's structure, these terms refer to an element (whether a character, piece of dialogue, or situation) being introduced early on, that then resolves later.

single camera scripts A script (usually for TV) intended to be shot with a single camera.

spec script Short for a speculative script, this is an unpaid script a writer hopes to sell eventually. This is opposed to a script that a writer is hired to write.

syndication Leasing the right to broadcasting television shows and radio programs to multiple television stations and radio stations, without going through a major network.

synopsis A succinct summary of a script's plot. It includes the main plot points and is very important when a reader must convey the story to an employer who has not read the project themselves.

tag This is a closing scene at the end of a TV script, usually in a sitcom. It's usually a last bit, gag, or character moment. The belief is that if it gets cut, it won't affect the main story.

teaser Similar to a cold open, teasers introduce information or a conflict that will be relevant to the rest of the episode. Teasers are used most often in dramatic shows.

templates (for coverage) Standard samples that companies often provide, listing the format and elements they want their readers to cover.

verbal notes When script notes and critiques on scripts are given orally.

written coverage When script notes and critiques are given in a written report, for companies or to writers themselves.

Index

A

Made in the USA
Las Vegas, NV
09 August 2022

52970997R10136